GUNS
AND CRIME

Other books in the At Issue series:

GUNS
AND CRIME

James D. Torr, *Book Editor*

Daniel Leone, *President*
Bonnie Szumski, *Publisher*
Scott Barbour, *Managing Editor*
Helen Cothran, *Senior Editor*

San Diego • Detroit • New York • San Francisco • Cleveland
New Haven, Conn. • Waterville, Maine • London • Munich

For more information, contact
Greenhaven Press
27500 Drake Rd.
Farmington Hills, MI 48331-3535
Or you can visit our Internet site at http://www.gale.com

LIBRARY OF CONGRESS CATALOGING-IN-PUBLICATION DATA
Guns and crime / James D. Torr, book editor.
p. cm. — (At issue)
Includes bibliographical references and index.
ISBN 0-7377-1998-2 (pbk. : alk. paper) — ISBN 0-7377-1997-4 (lib. : alk. paper)
1. Gun control—United States. 2. Firearms and crime—United States. I. Torr, James D., 1974– . II. At issue (San Diego, Calif.)
HV7436.G8772 2004
364'.042'0973—dc21   2003049147

Printed in the United States of America

Contents

Page

Introduction

The prevalence of guns in the United States and the frequency with which they are used to commit crimes have made gun control a much-discussed and contentious issue. There are an estimated 200 to 250 million firearms in America, and of these, about a third are handguns. According to health researcher Etienne Krug, the homicide rate in the United States is six times higher than that of other developed nations. And though it varies from year to year, according to the FBI, in general guns are used in about 70 percent of homicides. In 2000, for example, 52 percent of homicides were committed with handguns, and 19 percent were committed with other guns.

Crime vs. violence

An important distinction in the gun control debate is between gun *violence* and gun *crime*. Often these categories overlap. For example, there were twelve thousand gun homicides in 1998. Homicide is both violent and criminal, hence the term "violent crime." However, not all gun crime is violent crime—for example, armed robberies in which no one is hurt are criminal but not violent. Further confounding the issue is the fact that violent crimes are better documented—and therefore may be perceived as more widespread—than nonviolent crimes. This is because violent crimes, particularly homicide, are treated more seriously by law enforcement and are carefully investigated and documented. In contrast, reliable information on the number of gun crimes in which no shot was fired is much harder to obtain.

Moreover, not all gun violence is committed by criminals. For example, there were seventeen thousand gun suicides in 1998. Suicide is certainly a violent act, but it is generally not thought of as a criminal activity. There were also more than eight hundred fatal, but accidental, shootings in 1998—again, a type of gun violence that does not fit into most people's conception of gun crime.

"Gun violence" is a broader term than "gun crime" because it includes both gun homicides (which most people think of when they hear the term "gun crime") and gun suicides and accidental shootings (types of violence that most people do not associate with crime). Commentators on both sides of the gun control debate sometimes blur the distinction between gun crime and noncriminal gun violence in order to advance their own agendas—sometimes by using statistics on gun violence to exaggerate the problem of gun crime.

Antigun activists often use statistics on gun violence, rather than gun crime, in order to convince people that gun control laws are necessary. For example, the Brady Campaign to Prevent Gun Violence notes that "in 1998 alone, 30,708 Americans died from gunfire." This statistic is accurate, but because it combines the statistics on gun homicide, gun suicide, and accidental shootings, it may mislead people about the extent of gun crime (since more than half those who "died from gunfire" committed suicide or were victims of accidental shootings).

Conversely, opponents of gun control may use the more ominous statistics on gun violence to convince people that they need to purchase a handgun in order to protect themselves from ubiquitous gun-toting criminals. Those who accept this view would likely oppose any gun control legislation that would restrict the private ownership of guns. For example, pro-gun activists often argue that women should carry guns for self-defense. In doing so, they may cite the number of women "killed by" handguns and neglect to mention that many of those deaths were suicides or that the majority of rape and sexual assault victims do not face criminals armed with a gun.

Cause or deterrent?

While the various statistics on gun crime and violence can be used in confusing or misleading ways, the numbers are central to the gun control debate. Commentators on both sides of the issue argue about how often guns are used for self-defense in comparison to how often they are used to commit crimes. One of the main tenets of America's gun control movement is that reducing the availability of guns would reduce crime. Writing in the magazine *Christian Social Action*, United Methodist minister and gun control advocate C. Emory argues that:

> A number of studies confirm that the proportion of gun use in violence rises and falls with gun ownership. . . . In general, states with a high ownership of guns have a higher percentage of homicides using firearms. The simple fact is that murder and other crimes committed with firearms occur more frequently where gun control laws are least stringent. This applies both to the overall murder rate and to the percentage of murders involving firearms.

This position has, of course, been continually challenged by opponents of gun control. Pro-gun organizations such as the National Rifle Association (NRA) maintain that guns are an effective means of personal defense against criminals. In their view, gun ownership does not cause crime, but instead deters it. Florida State University criminologist Gary Kleck maintains that "gun use by private citizens against violent criminals and burglars is a more common negative consequence for violent criminals than legal actions like arrests, a more prompt negative consequence of crime than legal punishment, and is more severe, at its most serious, than legal system punishments." According to Kleck, "The best survey on defensive gun use frequency indicates 2.55 million defensive gun uses a year in the United States."

The guns-deter-crime argument received nationwide attention in 1998 with the publication of former University of Chicago economist John R. Lott Jr.'s book *More Guns, Less Crime*. In the book, Lott summarizes his analysis of eighteen years of national gun and crime data and concludes that states that allow citizens to carry concealed weapons have lower crime rates. Lott's research bolstered the view, long embraced by gun advocates, that criminals are less likely to act against potential victims that may be armed. While much of *More Guns, Less Crime* is devoted to detailed statistical analysis, Lott concludes his book on a provocative note: "Will allowing law-abiding citizens to carry concealed handguns save lives? The answer is yes, it will."

While Lott has become a hero of sorts for groups like the NRA, he and his research have come under a hail of criticism from gun control advocates. The primary criticism is that crime rates have been falling throughout the country for several years, and it is very difficult to show conclusively that one single factor, such as concealed-carry laws, is responsible for the decline. For example, in their book *Gun Violence: The Real Costs*, Philip J. Cook and Jens Ludwig contend that Lott "confounded the effects of concealed-carry laws with other factors" that may have reduced crime, and that "the best available evidence suggests that permissive concealed carry laws have little or no effect on violent crime and injuries."

Whether Lott's statistical analysis of concealed-carry laws is valid or not, many Americans find the logic behind Lott's conclusions appealing. The primary reason that people buy handguns is for self-defense, as evidenced by the sharp increase in guns sales in the weeks following the September 11, 2001, terrorist attacks on America. The popular belief that gun ownership may deter crime has become a significant obstacle to gun control legislation. As a result, many gun control advocates have shifted away from calls to ban handguns, instead focusing on policies that would reduce criminals' access to guns.

Keeping guns from criminals

One principle that both sides of the gun control debate agree on is that criminals should not own guns, but the two sides do not agree on how, or even if, this goal can be achieved. Noting America's high gun homicide rate in comparison to other developed nations, gun control advocates have looked to these nations as models for gun control policy. As social science professor Gregg L. Carter explains:

> Unlike the United States, most western European countries and other economically developed nations have strict national gun laws. These countries require that guns be registered, that gun owners be licensed, and that guns be stored and transported with utmost security. To get a license, a potential gun owner must typically pass an exam on gun safety. Also required are comprehensive background checks of individuals seeking to purchase guns, including any history of criminality or mental incapacity.

The United States only began implementing such a system with the 1993 Brady Law, which instituted mandatory background checks for gun purchasers in an effort to screen out ineligible gun buyers. The Brady Law, however, has drawn criticism from both sides of the gun control debate.

Gun control advocates point out, for example, that the Brady background check system is still very permissive in comparison to the European or Canadian systems in terms of who is deemed eligible to purchase a handgun. Gun control advocates also say that further legislation is necessary to close various "loopholes" in the Brady Law that enable criminals to buy guns. The most infamous is the so-called "gun show loophole," which allows unlicensed, private gun sellers to ignore the background check system.

Groups like the NRA, on the other hand, contend that the Brady Law is fundamentally flawed. They maintain that in terms of gun control, the United States is not comparable to other nations because Americans already have so many guns. In their view, instituting a background check system at this late stage in U.S. history will have little effect, since the law only affects sales of new guns. Even if the "gun show loophole" is closed through further legislation, they insist, criminals will still have easy access to the millions of guns that are already on the black market.

Both sides in the gun control debate have some valid arguments, and the passage of the Brady Law gives some hope that there is room for compromise. Gun control activists seem to be slowly coming to terms with the fact that the United States will not soon have a gun control system as restrictive as other countries', and a segment of gun rights activists are grudgingly conceding that background checks, while not a panacea, may stop at least some criminals from getting guns. Pro- and antigun groups are also finding some room for compromise in measures that aim to reduce gun violence—for example, mandatory gun safety training for first-time gun buyers and laws that punish parents who keep a gun in the home and fail to keep it securely out of their children's reach.

The viewpoints in *At Issue: Guns and Crime* provide a survey of current thinking on the relationship between guns and crime as well as an overview of the arguments surrounding gun control proposals. The pressure is now on both sides of the gun debate to devise new strategies for reducing gun crime and the broader problem of gun violence.

1

Gun Ownership Does Not Cause Violent Crime

Don B. Kates Jr.

Don B. Kates Jr. is a criminological policy analyst with the Pacific Research Institute in San Francisco and the coauthor, with Gary Kleck, of Armed: New Perspectives on Gun Control.

Gun control advocates are fond of claiming that guns are a major cause of homicide and other violent crimes, but there is no statistical data to support this conclusion. Rates of gun ownership increased at a much greater pace throughout the twentieth century than murder rates did, and from 1973 to 1997 murder rates declined significantly while rates of gun ownership increased. In shorter periods when both crime rates and rates of gun ownership increased, the likely explanation is that people bought guns in response to rising crime rates, not that gun purchases caused crime rates to increase.

Anti-gun advocates present their position as pragmatic and intellectually based, specifically as a program for eliminating the widespread ownership of firearms, a phenomenon they believe to be a (or the) major cause of murder in America. Despite this facade of rationalism, what the anti-gun position actually rests on is intellectual confusion, abetted, it must be said, by a credulous desire to believe. That desire alone explains how believers in the anti-gun faith credulously accept concepts they would instantly reject as absurd in any other context.

Consider the fallacious argument from correlation that so many otherwise intelligent and skeptical people credulously swallowed 30 years ago—and have since never reexamined. For a brief period in the 1960s and early 1970s, the American homicide rate and the number of firearms owned were both rapidly increasing at the same time. The argument seriously advanced then, and consistently maintained ever since by many anti-gun advocates, is that a correlation of more guns and more homicide proves that the widespread availability of guns is a primary cause of murder.

This is a simple-minded confusion of cause and effect. In the late 1970s, California State University economist Joseph Magaddino com-

Don B. Kates Jr., "Intellectual Confusions," *Handguns*, vol. 14, July 2000, p. 12. Copyright © 2000 by Petersen Publishing Company. Reproduced by permission.

pared it to a basketball team, noting the correlation that the temperature in the auditorium goes up when their games attract large numbers of spectators—and concluding that the way to attract more fans is to turn the heat up in the auditorium.

The fact is that a mere correlation between increases in gun buying and in homicide does not and cannot prove guns cause murder. Assuming that there is any cause and effect relationship, the most obvious one is the reverse, i.e., that it was the rise in murders that caused increased gun buying. Alternatively, the upsurges in both murders and gun sales may have been caused by a third factor, e.g., the enormous increase in burglary and violent crime that also began in the 1960s.

Taken either together or separately, these crime-causes-guns explanations are far more plausible than the guns-cause-murder explanation for the brief 1960–'70s correlation between increases in gun buying and in murder. It is virtually self-evident that people buy guns in response to dramatically increasing crime in general and murders in particular. Indeed, so clearly true is it that fear drives gun ownership that anti-gun advocates themselves agree—adding, however, that people's natural urge to protect their families should be prohibited because gun ownership is "the principal cause of murder."

Note that this guns-cause-murder notion is a bare speculation that is not supported by the brief 1960s–'70s correlation of more guns and more murder. That correlation fails to support the guns-cause-murder speculation because that correlation is independently explained by the accepted fact that people react to crime and violence by acquiring guns. Neither in the 1960s nor today is there intellectual support for the claim that guns are the "primary" cause of murder. The belief that there is such support is a mere intellectual confusion based on credulous desire to believe.

Neither in the 1960s nor today is there intellectual support for the claim that guns are the "primary" cause of murder.

Only that credulity, and/or sheer ignorance, explains how the anti-gun view continues today when decades of post-1960s evidence have reduced the anti-gun view from an unsupported speculation to a clearly erroneous one. This evidence arises from an unarguable point: If guns really were a (or the) primary cause of murder, an enormous increase in guns would necessarily lead to a more or less comparably large increase in the murder rate. The fact is that handgun ownership has increased about 3.5 times more than the population increase since the end of World War II—with no comparable increase in the murder rate.

Space does not permit detailed review of the statistics. Readers who are interested should consult the May 2000 issue of *Homicide Studies*, a criminology journal which will carry an article I co-authored with Professor Daniel Polsby. (An unrevised prepublication version may be found on my website, donkates.com.) Our article's findings include such facts as that the homicide rate decreased 27.7 percent over the 25-year period 1973–97 despite increases of 160 percent in the number of civilian handguns and of 103 percent in guns of all kinds. (These increases far outstripped the population increase over that period.)

It is important to emphasize the limitations on our findings. They should not be confused with the conclusion of Yale Law School economist John Lott that increasing firearms availability actually decreases violent crime, based on statistics from before and after 30 states enacted laws under which concealed carry licenses are issued to every qualified applicant, and comparisons to the states that have not enacted such laws. While we do not disagree with Professor Lott, his is a study of a specific law and is based on much more extensive data and a much more sophisticated methodology than ours. All our study does is discredit the theory that widespread gun ownership is a major cause of homicide. If that theory were valid, the enormous increases in guns over the post World War II period should have been—but were not—highly correlated with comparable homicide rate increases. Even more significant is that vast gun increases over the 25 most recent years coincided with a dramatic decrease in murder rates.

Ignoring the facts

It bears emphasis that the anti-gun movement's failure to deal with such data involves not just intellectual confusion but evasion and fraud. Please understand that our article is not some feat of arduous research into arcane data. Any competent scholar could have duplicated our data in less than a week; indeed, any intelligent layperson with access to a university library could have done so. Moreover, anti-gun groups like Handgun Control, Inc. (HCI) [renamed the Brady Campaign to Prevent Gun Violence in 2001] would not have needed our article to know the general pattern: Over the past 25 years the homicide rate exhibited only minor fluctuation, followed by substantial decline, despite a vast increase in the number of guns. Though our precise statistics would not be known, this general pattern is something anyone seriously interested in the relationship between guns and homicide would know.

If there were some way to reconcile that general pattern with the claim that widespread gun ownership is the primary cause of murder, surely someone would have announced it. Tellingly, since the mid-1970s anti-gun advocates have instead "supported" that claim with meaningless short-term homicide statistics. Remember that homicide rates are not static. It is easy for HCI, et al, to say, as they regularly have, things like "In 1978 and 1979, over 8 million more guns were added to the existing stock and homicide increased by X percent." Saying that is also meaningless. It is a mere fluctuation, since in 1976 and 1977, homicide decreased by a comparable amount despite the fact that over 8 million more guns were added to the existing stock in those years.

To even begin to show by correlation that guns are the (or even a) major cause of American homicide would require showing a long-term, consistent correlation: Twenty or 30 years in which vast increases in guns were paralleled by vast increases in the murder rate. The lack of any such consistent pattern dooms the notion that guns are a major cause of homicide. (The fact that the actual pattern is the reverse suggests the opposite conclusion which Professor Lott impressively supports with the data in his book *More Guns, Less Crime*.)

2

Gun Ownership Increases the Lethality of Violent Crime

Josh Sugarmann

Josh Sugarmann is director of the Violence Policy Center, a gun control advocacy organization, and the author of Every Handgun Is Aimed at You: The Case for Banning Handguns, *from which the following viewpoint is excerpted.*

When people think about gun homicides, they often imagine "street criminals"—strangers who murder their victims in the course of committing a robbery or rape. But in reality, the majority of homicides in America result from confrontations between two people who know each other. For example, most female homicide victims are killed by an intimate acquaintance. Handguns are the most common weapon used in homicides. Thus, while gun ownership does not cause people to commit violence, it dramatically increases the likelihood that violence will culminate in homicide.

The vast majority of gun death and injury—suicides and unintentional shootings—is not crime related. While there is growing public acceptance of gun violence as a public health issue, the vast majority of Americans still view the issue through the prism of crime. The most vivid image they have is that of a stranger, armed with a handgun, attacking them on a city street. And while the handgun is the preferred tool of crime for street thugs and murderers, the reality of handguns and crime is far more complex than it would seem at first glance and, . . . far more disturbing.

The core reality—which flies in the face not only of pro-gun rhetoric, but of images seen constantly in television and movies—is that the majority of homicides in America result from confrontations between people who know each other, and not from criminal attacks by strangers. Only a small percentage stems from circumstances related to "crime" as we ordinarily think of it, i.e., felonies such as criminal "hits," rape, assault, robbery, etc.

The reality of homicide in America

So if it is not the "street criminal" of our collective imaginations, just who is in fact committing most of these murders? Homicides are unique within the spectrum of gun violence because data regarding them are collected and reported in relatively extensive detail. Consequently, more information is available about homicide victims and offenders than for any other crime in which a handgun is involved. Through arrest data available from the Federal Bureau of Investigation's *Uniform Crime Reports* and its supporting databases, we can develop demographic profiles of the persons committing homicides, and of their victims. This information includes age, sex, relationship between victim and offender, and the circumstances in which shootings occur.

There were 14,772 homicides in the United States in 1998. The most common weapon used in these murders was no different than for any other year in the past generation: 9,755 murders, or nearly seven out of 10, were committed with firearms, and of those, four times out of five the murder weapon was a handgun. (To be exact, in 1998 there were 7,875 handgun homicides, which made up 80.7 percent of all murders in which a firearm was used.) Using a larger sample over a longer time period gives similar results: from 1990 to 1998, handguns were used not only in the vast majority of firearm homicides (81 percent) but in a majority of all homicides (55 percent). That is, handguns were used in murder more than *all other weapons combined*. There is really nothing out of the ordinary revealed here. Handguns have held center stage for as long as reliable murder statistics have existed.

As one might assume, of the 7,875 handgun homicides committed in 1998, when the victim/offender relationship could be identified, most involved a single victim being killed by a single offender (77.4 percent). The next largest group of homicide victims (18 percent) were slain by multiple offenders. Cases where a single shooter has claimed multiple victims compose approximately three percent of total homicides. Multiple victim/multiple offender incidents make up the remaining one percent.

For all homicides, two out of three victims had some sort of relationship with the person who took their lives. In contrast, 32.1 percent of all murder victims were killed by strangers. The larger of these two groupings, i.e., victims who knew their killers, is conventionally divided into three parts: intimate acquaintances, family, and "other." This is what the data show for handgun homicides:

- Seven out of 10 victims of handgun homicides were killed by someone in the "other" category, i.e., someone with whom they had a non-intimate relationship, such as a friend, acquaintance, or neighbor.
- More than one out of five handgun homicide victims were intimate acquaintances of the offender. (An intimate acquaintance is defined as a spouse, ex-spouse, common-law spouse, girlfriend/boyfriend, or homosexual partner.)
- One out of 12 of all handgun homicide victims were killed by family members.

When analyzing handgun homicide, it becomes clear that men and women don't die the same way. When dramatized on television, or when presented by those trying to market handguns to women, the deadliest threat to a woman is the stereotypical violent stranger lurking in an alley or just outside her bedroom window. Such predators do exist, but of all the women killed with handguns in 1998, only a surprisingly slim 12.5 percent were slain by strangers. In truth, the *greatest danger* to a woman comes from the men she knows best, as more than half of all female handgun homicide victims (57 percent) were killed by an intimate acquaintance. Among female homicide victims, an additional 6.8 percent were killed by family members using handguns, and 23.7 percent by persons more casually known to the victim.

Although, like women, most men (63.1 percent) are killed by people whom they know, those people are rarely intimate acquaintances. Fewer than one out of 20 (4.7 percent) male handgun homicide victims were killed by an intimate acquaintance in 1998. Only one out of 20 (5.2 percent) of 1998's male handgun homicide victims were killed by family members. The vast majority of men (53.2 percent) were killed by friends and acquaintances. Undoubtedly there are cases in which the "acquaintance" was someone known to the victim through questionable activities but, as is borne out by newspaper articles and coroners' reports, it is astonishing how often a male victim and shooter, up until the moment the trigger is pulled, consider themselves friends.

"Cracking down" on criminals does little to deter the violent spouse reaching for a gun in a spasm of irrationality.

Another false stereotype is the black criminal who preys almost solely on white suburban families or lone white women. These images of interracial crime, rape, and sexual assault, while rarely mentioned together— except by pro-gun listeners on radio call-in shows—form a consistent, unspoken subtext of self-defense arguments offered by gun manufacturers and pro-gun lobbying organizations. In reality, homicides are almost entirely intra-racial. Between 87 percent and 93 percent of all murderers are of the same race as their victims. Indeed, in 1998 the FBI reported that 94 percent of all black homicide victims were killed by black offenders, and that 87 percent of white victims were killed by white offenders.

By attempting to focus the blame on an easily identifiable group of "bad people," pro-gunners are trying to change the subject. They seek to obscure the reality that it is our outsized handgun population that guarantees that *all* people—good, bad, and in-between—have at hand the means to inflict lethal violence, at every level of our society. "Cracking down" on criminals does little to deter the violent spouse reaching for a gun in a spasm of irrationality, the driver succumbing to "road rage," the depressed lover desperate to end his life, or the misfit settling life's score in a random shooting. . . .

In the rhetorical battle over gun control, terms like " criminal" and "law-abiding" are bandied about with little precision. Most of us agree that "criminals" shouldn't have guns. But what exactly is a criminal?

Most laws on the ownership and sale of guns define a " criminal" as a person who has been convicted of a felony—that is, a crime calling for a sentence of at least one year in prison. Federal law, for example, bars felons from buying or even possessing firearms. For the most part, however, state and federal gun laws have ignored less serious crimes, usually called misdemeanors. There is growing evidence that this is a serious mistake.

Only when it comes to lethal *violence does the United States dramatically outpace other nations.*

Recently more attention has been paid at the federal level to a specific class of misdemeanor crimes—those involving domestic violence. Historically, domestic violence crimes have been treated as less serious by the judicial system. But faced with persuasive evidence that domestic violence often involves gun violence, Congress has passed several laws restricting access to firearms for those found to be involved in domestic violence. In 1994, Congress banned possession of firearms by persons under restraining orders (which are often issued to keep the violent partner away from the other). In 1996, the Domestic Violence Offender Gun Ban barred gun possession by those convicted of misdemeanor domestic-violence charges.

Ironically, the law treats as "law-abiding" even those chronic offenders who manage to avoid felony records by repeatedly plea-bargaining serious charges down to the misdemeanor level. As usual, the public is far ahead of Congress on this issue, with polls showing strong support for expanding the categories of persons prohibited from possessing guns.

Does a history of low-level, mostly nonviolent criminal activity serve as a red flag for serious trouble in the future? A 1998 study by Dr. Garen Wintemute found that a handgun buyer with only one misdemeanor conviction and no convictions for firearm offenses or violence was nearly *five times* as likely as a buyer with a clean record to be charged with new offenses involving firearms or violence. A handgun purchaser with one or more misdemeanor convictions was more than *seven times* as likely to be charged with a new offense after buying a handgun as was a buyer with no prior criminal history.

Crime is not the problem

In their groundbreaking 1997 book *Crime Is Not the Problem: Lethal Violence in America*, Franklin Zimring and Gordon Hawkins reveal that United States rates of nonviolent crime (burglary, theft, and other property crimes) are in fact comparable to those of other industrialized nations. This trend holds true not just for countries, but even for similar-sized cities, such as New York and London or Los Angeles and Sydney. Only when it comes to *lethal* violence does the United States dramatically outpace other nations. In comparing countries' homicide rates, Zimring and Hawkins note, "What is striking about the quantity of lethal violence in the United States is that it is a third world phenomenon occurring in a first world nation." The authors write:

Rates of common property crimes in the United States are

comparable to those reported in many other Western industrial nations, but rates of lethal violence in the United States are much higher than can be found elsewhere in the developed nations. This penchant for violence cannot be a natural result of a high volume of either crime or criminals. If it were, other developed nations with high crime rates would share our higher rate of violence. The propensity toward life-threatening violence varies independently of general crime rates.

Zimring and Hawkins . . . find that most gun homicides are not crime related. In discussing the catalytic role that firearms play in lethal violence, the authors conclude:

Current evidence suggests that a combination of the ready availability of guns and the willingness to use maximum force in interpersonal conflicts is the most important single contribution to the high U.S. death rate from violence. Our rate of assault is not exceptional; our death rate from assault is exceptional.

3

Stronger Gun Control Laws Can Help Reduce Crime

Steven Riczo

Steven Riczo is director of ambulatory operations at the University Hospitals Health System in Beachwood, Ohio.

The United States has higher levels of gun ownership than any other developed nation, and the highest gun homicide rate to match. The most common reason Americans cite for owning a handgun is to protect against crime, but guns are used in homicides, suicides, and unintentional shootings more than eleven times more often than they are used in self-defense. To reduce gun crime and violence Americans must embrace rational gun control policies, such as licensing of gun owners and registration of firearms, raising the legal age for possession of handguns to 21, legislating mandatory waiting periods for gun purchases, and requiring gun manufacturers to make their products safer.

As Americans become sickened by one firearm tragedy after another, the momentum may be building for a shift in the nation's approach to guns in the 21st century. While it is certainly true that the U.S. has had a tradition of gun ownership, much has changed since the days of the Wild West. This is the age of the Internet, instant global communications, medical marvels, genetic engineering, and other technological wonders that are transforming our lives. Citizens don't have to give up their fight to own firearms in order to make progress on this issue, but should approach it in a more intelligent manner than the bumper sticker mentality and oversimplistic slogans that have characterized this polarized debate. The real question we should be asking ourselves isn't whether or not the government should curtail the right to own firearms, but, as an American, do I really want to own one? Ownership rights can be balanced with reasonable limits in the quest for a sensible gun policy.

There are also interesting political ramifications in light of the razor-thin election of President George W. Bush. During the presidential race, there were many critics of then-Governor Bush who maintained that his

Steven Riczo, "Guns, America, and the 21st Century," *USA Today*, vol. 129, March 2001, p. 16.

policy positions are simply reflections of the special interests that contributed to his campaign, such as the National Rifle Association (NRA), defense contractors, the oil industry, etc. There were also frequent concerns raised that he may lack the intellectual wherewithal or was perhaps intellectually too lazy to analyze complex issues and then make a wise choice. The gun safety issue could be an interesting test of these assertions.

A widely viewed videotape showed an NRA official publicly boasting that, if Bush won the election, they would have their man in the White House. If the President is to demonstrate that he is a "compassionate conservative" he must carefully listen to all sides of an issue. There are groups other than the NRA that present opposing, yet compelling, arguments, such as the Coalition to Stop Gun Violence, supported by 44 well-respected national scientific, civic, and religious organizations, including the American Academy of Pediatrics, American Public Health Association, Center for Science in the Public Interest, United Federation of Teachers, and U.S. Conference of Mayors. If Bush's actions prove his critics right, he could lose support of many Americans who backed him the first time around.

The official Republican campaign website, Bush/Cheney 2000 Inc., promised Americans that Bush's policy on gun safety would protect citizens' constitutional rights "while at the same time enacting reasonable, common-sense restrictions on the unsafe use of firearms." It is incumbent upon the President and the nearly evenly split Congress to heed the voices of the majority who would like to see progress on this issue.

Other developed nations are willing to accept a reasonable compromise between ownership rights and common-sense restrictions and tend to view gun policy as part of an overall public health plan. The typical reaction of other developed nations to our frequent firearm tragedies is "only in America." The U.S. has the highest per capita gun ownership among all developed nations. The firearm violence comparisons between the U.S. and other industrialized countries are staggering. According to the Centers for Disease Control, the U.S., one of the richest nations on Earth, suffers "the highest firearm mortality rate." Americans murder each other with guns at a rate 19 times higher than any of the 25 richest nations surveyed by CDC. Since 1960, more than 1,000,000 Americans have died from firearm homicides, suicides, and accidental shootings. Moreover, for every firearm death, there are six nonfatal injuries.

Other developed nations are willing to accept a reasonable compromise between [gun] ownership rights and common-sense restrictions.

Americans own 200,000,000 guns, of which approximately 70,000,000 are handguns. One interesting feature of the high level of gun ownership is that it is not evenly distributed among its citizens. In the most extensive firearm survey ever conducted in the U.S., the National Institute of Justice found that 35% of households had guns present. Conversely, this also means that 65% of adults and heads of households have rejected gun ownership.

When asked why they chose not to own a gun, the most common

reasons identified were that such weapons are dangerous, "immoral" or otherwise objectionable. Of those who own guns, 46% said they do so for prevention of crime, while the majority cited recreational purposes such as hunting and target shooting. Gun owners predominantly identified the reason for the purchase of rifles as recreation and buying handguns for protection against crime. There is also a stark contrast between gun ownership by region of the country—in descending order, the South, West, Midwest, and Northeast. In Texas, for example, there are 68,000,000 guns, which equates to four for every man, woman, and child.

Americans who currently own guns or are contemplating purchasing one would be well-served by objectively evaluating data from reliable organizations such as the Federal Bureau of Investigation [FBI] and the Justice Department's Bureau of Justice Statistics [BJS]. Both have extensive data, including detailed interview information from victims of crime. Simply put, guns are designed to kill, and when you bring one into your home, you increase the risk to yourself and family members. According to the *New England Journal of Medicine*, guns kept in the home for self-protection are 22 times more likely to kill someone you know than to kill in self-defense. According to Physicians for Social Responsibility, when a gun is kept in the home, it is about three times as likely that a death will occur in that household.

The self-protection argument

How are Americans to reconcile the risks to themselves and family members of bringing a gun into the home vs. the odds that they will use the firearm to protect their own lives or property against an intruder? A review of the facts should provide some clarity on which to base a decision. First, interviews with detectives in various police departments revealed that about 90% of residential burglaries occur when the owner or family is not at home. The odds of an American being killed during a burglary is quite low, with 61 such deaths out of 14,088 homicides in 1998.

One also must consider the increased risk to the homeowner in pulling a gun on a felon who could have more firearm experience than the victim. As one Bureau of Alcohol, Tobacco, and Firearms [BATF] agent described in an interview, a law-abiding citizen pulling a gun for the first time to shoot a criminal is in a very difficult situation. He or she has now forced the hand of the perpetrator in a life-threatening and probably terrifying situation for the homeowner. Unless the homeowner has extensive and regular training in the use of firearms comparable to that received by law enforcement officers or the military, the odds of success are slim.

There were just 195 justifiable homicides in 1998 by private citizens out of more than 12,000,000 reported crimes in the U.S. The majority of justifiable killings are by law enforcement officers. According to the *Journal of the American Medical Association*, even when someone is home, a gun is used for protection in less than two percent of home-incursion crimes. Other nonfirearm options for protection against home incursion are available, such as dialing 911 (police will be dispatched even if you are not in a position to talk), buying a dog, or installing a burglar alarm system with monitoring by a protective services company.

On any given day, 1,100,000 Americans carry concealed weapons on them outside the workplace, and 2,100,000 in their vehicles. The rate is twice as high in the South as the rest of the nation. FBI data show that just 0.6% of violent-crime victims used a firearm in an attempt to defend themselves. According to the Bureau of Justice Statistics (BJS) National Crime Utilization Survey, 29% of violent-crime victims faced an offender with a gun. Of those, three percent suffered gunshot wounds. In other words, even if you are unfortunate enough to face an assailant with a firearm, there is a 97% chance that you will not be shot. BJS surveys from a number of years consistently indicate that about 85,000 crime victims use guns in an attempt to protect themselves or their property out of a total of 13,000,000 reported crimes (FBI) or 40,000,000 crimes, including unreported ones (Justice Department). Either way, guns are used in defense in less than one percent of crimes committed.

The BJS victim interviews reveal that, in 72% of violent crimes, victims take some self-protective measures, but more than 98% of those acts do not include the use of a firearm. For instance, in 10% of cases, the victim attacked the perpetrator without using a weapon; nine percent scared off the offender; nine percent got help or sounded an alarm; 16% ran or hid; 13% persuaded or appeased the offender; 2.4% screamed; 1.7% threatened the offender with a weapon; and 1.5% threatened the offender without a weapon. Clearly, self-preservation methods without the use or threat of use of a weapon comprise the vast majority of cases. Sixty-five percent of those who employed some type of self-preservation method said their actions either helped avoid injury, scared off the offender, and/or enabled them to escape the situation or protect their property. Just nine percent of those who took self-protective measures said those actions made the situation worse.

There have been some gun ownership advocates who have exaggerated the extent by which ordinary citizens protect their lives and property with firearms. One widely quoted concealed weapons study concluded that violent-crime incidents declined in states that had passed right-to-carry (concealed weapons) laws. The full truth is that violent crime has decreased in every region of the country, regardless of gun ownership laws. FBI crime data indicates that, in the seven states that the NRA identifies as having the most-restrictive concealed weapons laws on the books, homicides/non-negligent manslaughter declined in six of them between 1993 and 1999—Illinois, Kansas, Missouri, Nebraska, Ohio, and Wisconsin. The 11 states identified as having moderately restrictive concealed weapons laws all experienced homicide declines. For example, per 100,000 inhabitants, Missouri declined from 11.3 to 6.6; Ohio, from six to 3.5; and California and New York both experienced dramatic declines from approximately 13 to six and five, respectively.

Gun homicides and suicides

U.S. homicide rates historically have been characterized by wide fluctuations, being relatively high in the 1920s and 1930s, much lower in the 1940s and 1950s, and then high again for much of the last half-century, although showing favorable declines in recent years. For every time a citizen used a firearm in a justifiable homicide, 131 lives were ended in a firearm murder, suicide, or unintentional shooting. Law enforcement statistics and interviews show that approximately 45% of homicides were perpetrated by assailants related to or acquainted with their victim. Fifty-six percent of gun homicides resulted from arguments. Of all violent crime, 23% of offenders were family members and 48% acquaintances. Situations of family strife with the potential for domestic violence is a factor that should be kept in mind by any prospective gun owner.

Guns are used in defense in less than one percent of crimes committed.

Gun ownership also has a correlation with suicide. According to the National Institutes of Mental Health, 19,000,000 Americans suffer some form of depression each year, with up to 20% of untreated cases choosing suicide. While there are other developed countries without high gun ownership with suicide rates higher than the U.S., firearms are the most lethal choice of suicide options. According to Physicians for Social Responsibility, 84 people die every day in America by suicide, and 50 of those are by firearms. The risk of suicide is five times greater in households with guns.

The 1994 Police Foundation Survey revealed that the average gun owner had had his or her firearm for 13 years. When evaluating a gun purchase, prospective buyers should consider the length of time they will own their gun in the context of the normal ups and downs that people face over the course of many years, including depression over a job loss or loved one, family fights, divorce, or a bout with alcohol and/or drugs.

There is an additional risk of teen suicide in homes with firearms and, according to the Surgeon General, five percent of youngsters between the ages of nine and 17 have a diagnosis of a major depression, with 10–15% having some symptoms of depression. Suicidal adolescents are 75 times more likely to commit suicide when a gun is kept in the home. Impulsiveness appears to play an important role in suicide, especially youth suicide. It is not uncommon for adolescents to have passing suicidal tendencies. Youth who attempt suicide rarely have a clear and sustained desire to die.

Guns, of course, are not the sole reason for violent crime and suicide in the U.S. Many experts agree that gun violence results from intertwined complex causes, such as family problems, neighborhood concerns, drug/alcohol abuse, media gun violence, school/work pressures, poverty, and accessibility to guns. Some have pointed to the fact that America is a heterogeneous society compared to others with lower rates of violence. However, the fact remains that 94% of black murders in the U.S. were by black offenders, and 87% of white murders were by white offenders. Special attention must be given to violence among blacks. Although African-Americans make up 12% of the population, 47% of all murder victims are black. According to FBI data, 35% of murder offenders were white, 35% black, and 28% unknown. Poverty and low education also have a correlation with violent crime.

A comparison between Department of Commerce statistics and FBI Uniform Crime Report data on murder and non-negligent manslaughter shows that states with lower-than-average high school graduation rates and lower-than-average per capita income consistently have higher homicide rates. A number of southern states bear these characteristics, and, when combined with a high percentage of gun ownership, there is an increase in the propensity for violence with fatal consequences.

Violence-reduction policies must be multi-faceted and include better education, domestic violence reduction, improvement of the plight of the urban poor, the cutting of drug/alcohol abuse (35% of violent crime victims said the perpetrator had been drinking), early mental health intervention, and increased parental involvement with children. Guns should not be viewed as the sole cause of violence, but as an important contributing factor. While there are other weapons used in violent crimes, guns are used in 65% of homicides and 59% of all suicides. Guns create a distance from the violent act compared to other weapons/actions, such as knives, strangulation, beatings, or use of blunt objects, which are visibly more violent and sometimes riskier for the perpetrator. It is simply too easy in today's society to pull the trigger to end a temporary episode of depression or rage.

Controlling guns

It is within America's power to start moving toward a more rational approach to firearms. Gun-control proposals often include the following elements:

- Raising the legal age for the possession of handguns from 18 to 21
- Limiting handgun purchases so that no individual is able to buy more than one gun per month
- Holding parents legally accountable when their children commit crimes with guns that they obtained as a result of the negligent storage of the weapons and ammunition
- Improving the design and manufacture of firearms, including installing child-locks, personalizing a gun so that it can only be fired by its owner, and adding load indicators that tell the user that the gun is still loaded or magazine-disconnect safeties which prevent the gun from firing if the ammunition magazine is removed
- Applying restrictions on gun manufacturers who produce low-quality, easily concealable "junk guns" or Saturday night specials and strict regulations against cop-killer bullets and mail-order parts that allow individuals to assemble untraceable guns
- Educating consumers about the true risks and rewards of gun ownership for enhanced personal safety
- Prohibiting gun advertisements in publications with substantial youth readership and including warnings about the risks of guns in the home
- Altering distribution and sales practices by improving security systems to avoid theft from dealers, prohibiting straw purchases by gun traffickers who then resell guns on the streets to criminals, closing gun show loopholes, and legislating mandatory waiting periods
- Federal licensing of handgun owners and registration of the handguns.

Licensing of handgun owners and registration of the handgun itself deserves special mention, as it has been the cornerstone of handgun responsibility and accountability throughout most of the developed world, including Australia, Austria, Belgium, Brazil, Canada, Finland, France, Germany, Great Britain, Greece, Hong Kong, India, Ireland, Israel, Italy, Japan, Malaysia, Mexico, the Netherlands, New Zealand, Northern Ireland, Norway, the Philippines, Portugal, Russia, Singapore, Slovakia, Sweden, and Switzerland. The U.S. does not have mandatory owner licensing and registration of handguns, with the exception of a handful of states and a few cities that have some components. Hawaii, where handguns have been registered for 40 years, has tight restrictions on carrying concealed weapons and a gun-death rate one-third the national average.

Around the world, handgun registration and owner licensing are acknowledged as the most effective way to minimize handgun-related death and trauma.

Philip Alpers, a highly credentialed gun-policy researcher, testified at the Select Committee on Gun Violence in California that, around the world, handgun registration and owner licensing are acknowledged as the most effective way to minimize handgun-related death and trauma. Effective registration of firearms acts to reduce the flow of guns from lawful owners to criminals. Computerized firearm registries are consulted thousands of times each day in some nations as a crime-busting tool.

Some of the common components of licensing and registration in developed nations are reviewing criminal history, domestic violence, and mental health; gun owner training, including public safety education as a condition of licensing; demonstrated need for a handgun; club membership with regular attendance required, such as an approved pistol club; interviewing the applicant's current or most recent spouse; secure storage requirements with the handgun and ammunition stored separately; verification of storage through physical inspections; fraud-resistant licensing procedures, such as requiring a thumbprint or photograph; limitations on ammunition that can be purchased for the type of firearm declared; mandatory removal of firearms within 24 hours of a domestic protection order; and regular reviews of gun owners for reapplication and periodic interviews.

Gun-control laws in the U.S. vary widely between states, but America has been willing to pass federal legislation when circumstances dictated. The nation's first major gun law was the Gun Control Act of 1968, passed in the wake of the assassinations of civil rights leader Martin Luther King, Jr., and Senator Robert Kennedy earlier that year. It established categories of prohibited purchasers, including convicted felons, fugitives from justice, minors, individuals with a history of mental illness, dishonorably discharged veterans, expatriates, and illegal aliens. It also set standards for gun dealers and age guidelines for gun purchasers. The Brady Handgun Violence Prevention Act that went into effect in February, 1984, required a five-day waiting period and background check before completion of the sale of a handgun. The five-day waiting period for handgun purchasers changed in November, 1998, to a computerized National Instant Check System, which provides the information for criminal background checks on all firearm purchasers. Current federal law focuses on small prohibited groups, but can provide the foundation for a comprehensive policy of education and training for all those who choose to own firearms.

It is time not to prohibit law-abiding citizens from owning a gun, but to be sure that they have correct factual data so that each can make an intelligent, informed choice pertaining to firearm ownership and then act responsibly after the purchase. Public policy should be geared to keeping firearms out of the hands of youth and to provide tools to trace firearms used in crimes to the original sources who are illegally providing firearms to criminals and young people. Continued tough enforcement of laws governing the use of firearms in the commission of a crime, coupled with a rational policy for law-abiding Americans, would be a major step in the right direction. In the area of gun policy, it is time to learn from the experiences of other developed nations in a manner that preserves individual rights, improves informed consumer choice, and encourages responsibility and accountability.

4

Stronger Gun Control Laws Will Not Reduce Crime

Linda Gorman and David B. Kopel

Linda Gorman is a senior fellow and David B. Kopel is the research director at the Independence Institute in Golden, Colorado.

Antigun activists frequently point to other nations to show that gun control laws can reduce crime, but in reality other nations' experiments with gun control have provided lessons in why gun control does not work. Japan's restrictive gun control laws have been successful in keeping crime down only because of the Japanese tradition of obedience to the government, and thus are not a model for the United States. Great Britain more closely resembles the United States in terms of demographics and culture, and its gun control efforts have been a disaster: British rates of assault and robbery are twice those of the United States, and since 1995 British homicide rates have risen while those in the United States have declined. Canada and Australia have followed the British model with similarly harmful results. The lesson from other nations is clear: Gun control laws empower criminals and leave ordinary citizens defenseless.

Reliable, durable, and easy to operate, modern firearms are the most effective means of self-defense ever devised. They require minimal maintenance and, unlike knives and other weapons, do not depend on an individual's physical strength for their effectiveness. Only a gun can allow a 110-pound woman to defend herself easily against a 200-pound man. Yet despite the superiority of firearms as a means of self defense, citizens in different countries, indeed in the 50 states of the United States, face a wide variety of obstacles—from restrictive licensing to outright bans—to buying, owning, or using guns.

Two competing philosophies govern the private ownership of firearms. In nations where government has historically derived its powers from the consent of the governed, as in the United States and Switzerland, guns have been relatively lightly regulated and are owned by size-

Linda Gorman and David B. Kopel, "Self-Defense: The Equalizer," *Forum for Applied Research and Public Policy*, vol. 15, Winter 2000, p. 92. Copyright © 2000 by Linda Gorman and David B. Kopel. Reproduced by permission.

able segments of the population. In nations where a central authority grants privileges to people, by history or custom, private firearms are subject to strict control or banned entirely.

Because it is impossible to abolish crime, governments that make guns illegal force law-abiding citizens to choose between protecting themselves and their loved ones or obeying the law. Jeffrey R. Snyder, author of "Fighting Back: Crime, Self-Defense, and the Right to Carry a Handgun," argues that

> a state that deprives its law-abiding citizens of the means to effectively defend themselves is not civilized but barbarous, becoming an accomplice of murderers, rapists, and thugs and revealing its totalitarian nature by its tacit admission that the disorganized, random havoc created by criminals is far less a threat than are men and women who believe themselves free and independent, and act accordingly.

In countries with strict bans on firearms, when people choose to disregard the law and carry guns for self-defense, governments trying to enforce the law tend to turn political disagreements into theater by characterizing this violation of the law as a moral failing. This threatens individual liberty. As the authors of *The Black Book of Communism* document, Communist states invariably degenerated into blood-soaked terror because those who ran them had the power to exclude those who did not agree with them. Anyone who did not agree with the reigning ideology was

> first labeled an enemy, and then declared a criminal, which leads to his exclusion from society. Exclusion very quickly turns into extermination. . . . After a relatively short period, society passes from the logic of political struggle to the process of exclusion, then to the ideology of elimination, and finally to the extermination of impure elements. At the end of the line, there are crimes against humanity.

When it's illegal to possess the means to protect one's family, the needs of individuals are subordinated to the political wishes of the government.

Fudging facts

Many governments are currently experimenting with stricter controls over the purchase, possession, and use of firearms. While these countries have little in common politically or economically with Communist states, they share a tendency of Communist countries to demonize one segment of society: gun owners. Their gun-control programs portray gun owners as the enemy, criminalize their behavior, and paint those who would defend themselves as beyond the moral pale. Moreover, these governments energetically suppress facts showing that gun possession does reduce crime and that gun control fails to do so. In the late 1990s, the Canadian Department of Justice, for example, squelched an independent report it had commissioned on the efficacy of Canadian gun laws because the data from its own report proved that Canadian gun laws had not reduced crime. And in 1996, after a gunman armed with a semiautomatic handgun shot and killed 16 children in a schoolyard in Dunblane, Scotland, the British Home Office misled the Dunblane Enquiry commission with false claims about comparative rates of international gun violence.

Gun-control advocates invariably promise that their measures will reduce crime rates and reduce the incidence of suicides. In the United Kingdom, Japan, Canada, and Australia, which either have or are introducing strict gun bans, the promised benefits have failed to materialize and, in fact, crime has increased. Frustrated governments have reacted by expanding the firearms ban to other weapons, including pocket knives. They have also authorized major expansions in the search and seizure powers of the police. These so-called reasonable gun-control measures progressively erode the traditional limits on police powers.

Such compromises can ultimately corrupt the government itself. Just how far democratic governments will progress down the slippery slope of eliminating basic civil rights in their quixotic quest to control gun ownership is anybody's guess, but there are few grounds for optimism. In the words of the late Nobel Laureate George Stigler, "government never knows when to quit."

The shogun state

Gun-control advocates frequently cite low Japanese crime and homicide rates as proof that gun control can work. In fact, they have things exactly backwards. Japanese society is the result of centuries of emphasis on subordinating individual interests to those of society, and an intricate web of social controls has been developed to ensure cooperative behavior.

Those same social controls may also contribute to Japan's extraordinarily high suicide rates—twice the U.S. level. There are indeed tradeoffs implicit in utopian gun-control proposals. And in spite of strict gun-control laws, murder rates in Japan are as high or higher than in Switzerland, where adult males are required by law to keep arms and ammunition for purposes of national defense.

Though American proponents of gun control believe that eliminating one method of suicide will reduce the total number of suicides, the high suicide rate in Japan does not support this claim. In fact, Japan and Switzerland have such high suicide rates that deaths in those countries from violent crime and suicide combined are higher than those of Australia, England and Wales, Canada, and the United States.

Guns were imported into Japan by Portuguese trading ships in 1542 or 1543. By 1575, the dictator Nobunaga had used a peasant army armed with matchlock guns—the first gun to use a mechanical device to light the gun-powder—to conquer most of Japan. Hideyoshi, who took control of the army after Nobunagas's death and set about reunifying Japan's feudal states under a strong central government, issued a decree in 1588 banning the private possession of "any swords, short swords, bows, spears, firearms, or other arms." Hideyoshi apparently understood, like the American Founders, that an armed citizenry would serve as a check on over-reaching government. According to Hidéyoshi, "the possession of unnecessary implements makes difficult the collection of taxes and tends to foment uprisings."

By 1650, Japan's *bakuhan* system had developed to give the shogun complete control. Villages were required to form five-household groups, essentially neighborhood associations to [according to the *Encyclopaedia Britannica*] "foster joint responsibility for tax payment, to prevent offenses against the laws of their overlords, to provide one another with mutual assistance, and to keep a general watch on one another." Families demanded absolute obedience to the household head. Japan's first constitution, completed in 1889, reflects the general reverence for the centralized state. It took the form of a gracious grant by the emperor, and could only be amended by imperial initiative. Rights and liberties were allowed "except as regulated by law." The rewriting of imperial education policy in 1890—making respect for the government part of the curriculum—was designed to guarantee that future generations would never question imperial authority.

With a history like this, it comes as no surprise that Japanese citizens see nothing wrong with laws that impose onerous licensing requirements on would-be owners of shotguns or air guns and entirely forbid the private ownership of handguns and swords. Rifles have been prohibited since 1971, and existing rifles must be turned in when the owner dies. Obtaining a shotgun or air gun license requires classes and a written test, shooting-range classes and a shooting test, a safety exam, a mental test at a local hospital, and a medical certificate certifying that the applicant is mentally healthy and not addicted to drugs. The classes are offered only during working hours so people must take time off to attend. Police investigate the families and background of license applicants and have unlimited discretion to deny a license for any reason. Membership in certain political or activist groups is deemed an instant disqualifier.

Gun control advocates invariably promise that their measures will reduce crime rates [but] . . . the promised benefits have failed to materialize.

Gun owners who successfully complete the licensing obstacle course must maintain a locker for the gun and a separate safe for ammunition. They must provide police with a map of their apartment giving the location of their gun safe and submit to annual home inspections at the whim of the police. Licenses must be renewed every three years, and renewal requires the owner to spend another day at police headquarters.

Widely respected and blessed with unparalleled cooperation from the citizenry, the Japanese police have few checks on their power. Neighborhood police visit the home of each gun owner twice a year, recording, among other things, how the occupants are related to one another, where they work, how late they stay out, what their finances are, and what kind of car they drive. The police keep lists of girls believed to have engaged in sexual misconduct. Police may search the belongings of suspicious characters at will, illegally seized contraband may be used as evidence, suspects may be detained for 28 days before seeing a judge, and according to the Tokyo Bar Association, the judiciary is uninterested in the fact that police routinely use torture or other illegal means to obtain confessions.

Japan's demographic homogeneity and extensive network of social controls may account for a low rate of reported violent crime, although that rate has risen notably in recent years. Yet criminals still have guns, and that concerns the Japanese police. According to the Firearms Division of the National Police Agency, police seize more than 1,000 illegal handguns every year, at least some of which are smuggled in. During the first half of 2000, there were reportedly 87 serious crimes involving guns—a 26 percent increase over the same period in 1999.

Japan's low violent crime rate may also be due to its ability to institutionalize crime. Some observers argue that political corruption in Japan is rampant and that organized crime has close links with legitimate enterprises. Like any other business, organized crime recognizes that random disorder on the streets is bad for profits. In a country where members of criminal organizations carry business cards, crime syndicates may contribute more to the low crime rate than gun control.

Crime in the kingdom

Unlike the Japanese, the British government has a long history of trusting common citizens to bear arms for their own defense and the defense of the nation. It also has a long history of taking those arms away from common citizens whenever the government felt threatened. In 1285, in response to rising crime throughout his kingdom, King Edward I enacted the Statute of Winchester requiring all males to own weapons. In 1539, King Henry VIII found that his fear of France outweighed his fear of crime and reversed his earlier command prohibiting anyone but the wealthy from owning a handgun or crossbow, the weapons favored by criminals.

In 1642, a militia loyal to Parliament had prevailed over the King's forces in Brentford. After the Restoration, the monarchy and a compliant Parliament attempted to disarm 95 percent of the population—ostensibly to prohibit hunting by commoners—with the Game Act of 1671. The law authorized daytime searches of any home suspected of containing an illegal gun; nevertheless, people chose to break the law. In 1685, the Catholic king, James II, commanded "a strict search to be made for such [illegal] muskets or guns and to seize and safely keep them till further order."

After James II was driven from the country in the Glorious Revolution of 1688–1689, the 1689 Bill of Rights reaffirmed that "the subjects which are Protestants may have arms for their defense suitable to their conditions as and allowed by law." This established a custom that was followed for the next two centuries. The only exception—a response to the tumultuous civil disorder that followed the Napoleonic War—was the Seizure of Arms Act of 1820, which expired in 1822 and applied to only a few counties. British subjects were armed in Britain while the British government, even when the first police force was established in 1829, was not.

Reversal of fortune

At the beginning of the 20th century, Great Britain was much like the United States in the 1950s. There were almost no gun laws and almost no gun crime. While the annual homicide rate was much lower than today—between 1.0 and 1.8 per 100,000 people—Parliament developed an interest in gun control because of rising unrest in the working classes and uninformed press hysteria over technological innovations in firearms, such as new revolvers that were "more dangerous than the bomb." With the Pistols Act of 1903, Parliament once again asserted its authority to control private firearms ownership. The act required buyers to pay a fee to obtain a license at the post office and forbade the sale of pistols to minors and felons.

In the aftermath of World War I and the Bolshevik Revolution, governments around the world took strong steps to secure themselves against revolution. In the United Kingdom, the Firearms Act of 1920 banned CS spray canisters marketed as tear gas for self-defense and allowed British citizens to possess pistols and rifles only if they could show a "good reason" for obtaining a permit. Publicly, the bill was presented as a measure to prevent the criminal misuse of guns. This was the first of many lies to make gun control palatable. In fact, the government was anxious to regulate its subjects because it did not trust them. At a Cabinet meeting on January 17, 1919, the chief of the Imperial General Staff raised the threat of "Red Revolution and blood and war at home and abroad" and suggested that the government make sure the military and police were adequately armed to resist an uprising. The next month, the prime minister wondered if some elements of the army would remain loyal. The Cabinet discussed arming university men, stockbrokers, and trusted clerks—a presumed economic and intellectual aristocracy—to fight any revolution.

Having established the principle that the state was free to regulate firearms and other weapons, the British government proceeded to provide a textbook demonstration of the proposition that government never knows when to quit. In 1936, it outlawed short-barreled shotguns and fully automatic firearms even though no one could cite a single instance of a machine gun being misused in the United Kingdom.

The police, who control the permit process, began adding storage requirements, although Parliament had never enacted such a requirement. Today, if a British citizen wants to obtain or renew a gun license, two police officers will visit his home to scrutinize the gun-security system. Although the law, even today, does not order guns to be locked in a safe, the police routinely compel gun owners to purchase safes—sometimes two safes, the second one for separate storage of ammunition. A man buying a low-powered, inexpensive rimfire rifle—commonly used for target shooting or small game—may have to spend 20 times the gun's value on a safe. A person with five guns may be ordered to add an electronic security system costing thousands. One effect of the heavy security costs is to make it hard for middle-income or poor people to legally own guns—an objective similar to Henry VIII's crossbow and handgun ban.

Following the fall of Dunkirk, the British government was so short of firearms it imported thousands from the United States and distributed them to its home defense forces. A fearful government collected and destroyed these weapons after the war, along with any gun brought in by returning servicemen. People caught bringing guns home were punished. In 1946, the home secretary announced that self-defense would no longer be considered a good reason for being granted a firearms certificate.

When three policemen were murdered with illegal handguns in 1966, Home Secretary Roy Jenkins, an ardent opponent of capital punishment, diverted public enthusiasm for the death penalty by initiating legislation to "do something about crime." The "something" was a licensing system for shotgun owners. Only six weeks earlier, Jenkins had told Parliament that shotgun controls were not worth the trouble.

Besides imposing the licensing system, the 1967 Criminal Justice Act eroded civil liberties by abolishing the requirement of unanimous jury verdicts in criminal trials, eliminating the requirement for a full hearing of evidence at committal hearings and restricting press coverage of those hearings.

The act further constrained legal self-defense by making it illegal to use a firearm against a violent home intruder. In one recent notorious case, in the summer of 2000, an elderly man, who had been repeatedly burglarized and had received no real help from the police, shot a pair of career burglars—killing one—who had broken into the man's home. The man was sentenced to life in prison.

In 1973, the Heath government proposed even more stringent controls. These far-reaching proposals, which mobilized protests from British shooting associations, were temporarily shelved. Since then, successive administrations have adopted the tactic of advancing most of the 1973 repressive proposals by disguising them as " doing something" during the hysterical reaction that typically follows a particularly sensational crime. In 1988, for example, Michael Ryan shot 16 people to death and killed himself in Hungerford, a small, quiet town in southern England. Ryan, who had permits for a wide variety of firearms, used a Beretta pistol as well as rifles in the killings.

The British government has refused to face the fact that crime has become worse as gun control has expanded.

Parliament quickly moved to restrict all types of firearms by passing the 1988 Firearms Act, which made shotgun licenses much more difficult to obtain. Self-loading centerfire rifles were easily confiscated thanks to previous legislation calling for registration and in-house inspection of all rifles and handguns. Home Secretary Douglas Hurd later admitted that the government had prepared the provisions of the 1988 Firearms Act long before Hungerford occurred and was waiting for the right moment of public hysteria to introduce them.

In 1996, this cycle of action and repression was repeated when Thomas Hamilton used handguns to murder 17 people at a kindergarten in Dunblane, Scotland. Hamilton was a licensed handgun owner who retained his license even though the police had investigated him seven times as a pederast and knew him to be mentally unstable. Pandering to a population unaccustomed to using firearms and uneducated about the different types and uses of guns, the Home Office and the newspapers used bogus statistical arguments to pound away at the theme that, since guns were unnecessary, anyone who owned one was mentally aberrant and presumably dangerous. Opponents of a handgun ban were denounced as accomplices in the murder of school children. All legally owned handguns were confiscated.

Rise in crime

Unfortunately, the British government's single-minded devotion to eliminating defensive arms has made life more dangerous for British citizens. In the United States, felons are more afraid of running into an armed homeowner than the police. As a result, the hot burglary rate—the rate of crimes that occur when the householder is home—is 13 percent in the United States and about 50 percent in England and Wales.

While imposing ever-stricter gun-control laws that disarm law-abiding citizens, the British government has done little to punish criminals. From 1981 to 1995, the rate of convictions rose in the United States while falling in England—for example, in the United States, conviction rates per 1,000 allegations for murders rose 43 percent, while in England, conviction rates for murders fell 12 percent.

Additionally, police in England and Wales were far less likely than U.S. police to even record crimes that were brought to their attention. In the United States, police record all of the assaults and an estimated 78 percent of the robberies reported to them. In England, police record just 53 percent of the known assaults and 35 percent of the known robberies.

Although the gun-control crusade has reduced the number of legal firearms in the United Kingdom, criminals can arm themselves from an illegal stockpile estimated to include 3 million weapons. Criminals know that guns in general, and rapid-fire weapons in particular, reduce their risk of failure by giving them better control over unarmed victims than do knives or blunt instruments. One of the more brazen incidents took place on August 3, 2000. Court officials dove for cover as a gang of armed men walked into a magistrate court in Slough, a small town just outside of London, fired at the ceiling, and walked out with the three men who had been in the dock facing charges of burglary.

In some areas like Manchester, called "Gunchester" by the police, criminals aged 15 to 25 years old have easy access to everything from Beretta sub-machine guns to Luger pistols. Detective Superintendent Keith Hudson of the national crime squad believes that increasingly criminals are choosing automatic weapons rather than pistols, since the police "are recovering weapons that are relatively new—and sometimes still in their boxes—from eastern European countries."

In fact, violent crime has risen steeply as British gun-control law has expanded. In 1981, England and Wales had lower rates of robbery and burglary than the United States. Assault and motor vehicle theft rates were only slightly higher. By 1995, a U.S. Department of Justice study concluded that rates of assault, burglary, robbery, and motor vehicle theft were roughly twice as high in the United Kingdom as in the United States. Homicide rates remained higher in the United States, as they were even before either country had any form of gun control, but the gap was beginning to close. While U.S. homicide rates are likely overstated by 10 percent—because U.S. homicide data record homicide arrests rather than homicide convictions—rates have declined in recent years as British rates have risen.

The British government has refused to face the fact that crime has become worse as gun control has expanded; instead, it has concentrated on extending the firearms laws to include control of other weapons, even including pen-knives. Law-abiding citizens who violate even the most obscure portion of the increasingly complex firearms law, even when they are defending themselves, are charged and jailed. The criminals go free. One elderly lady, for example, tried to frighten off a gang of thugs by firing a blank from her imitation firearm. She was arrested and charged with "putting someone in fear with an imitation firearm." Her attackers went free.

In 1996, knife carrying was made presumptively illegal. The government arrested and jailed Dean Payne, a man who worked in a newspaper distribution plant and carried a knife to cut the straps used to hold newspaper bundles, for carrying an "offensive weapon." In the words of the magistrate, "I have to view your conduct in light of the great public fear of people going around with knives. . . . I consider the only proper punishment is one depriving you of your liberty."

With hindsight it is easy to see how the United Kingdom's approach to gun control brought it to the point where an individual newspaper cutter can be jailed for adding to public fear. Successive government officials began with the false proposition that certain "reasonable regulations" controlling guns in the hands of the law abiding would reduce the criminal use of guns. When the expected results failed to materialize, the governments used the standard argument to defend any failing program—to see results, we need stiffer regulations and more resources. When the public resisted increased regulation, gun-control advocates ignored research that undermined their position, used horrific anecdotes to stoke public fears, and manipulated the resulting public hysteria. Gun ownership for self-defense is prohibited, handguns confiscated, and rifles and shotguns severely restricted; yet there is no reduction of crime in sight, and innocent people are now imprisoned as a frustrated bureaucracy continues to extend its reach.

Canadian confiscation

Although firearms regulations in Canada and Australia have historically been moderate, both nations in recent years have aggressively implemented the British model, with similar results. In 1920, in the midst of public hysteria over a Winnipeg general strike in which one marcher was killed and 30 were injured, the Canadian Parliament passed a bill mandating that residents obtain a permit to purchase any kind of gun. In 1921, when things had calmed down, the law was modified. Permits were required only to carry or purchase handguns. Handgun registration was imposed in 1934.

Long guns—rifles and shotguns—in Canada were subject to hardly any control at all. In 1940, a government effort to register long guns, under the pretext of World War II, failed. No more than one-third of gun owners cooperated and registered their guns. The effort was abandoned in 1945.

The first modern round of regulation occurred in response to two incidents in 1976 in which boys with rifles ran amok in public schools. A 1977 law required that gun purchasers get a Firearms Acquisition Certificate from the police. Changes in the law in 1995 gave the police the discretion to reject any applicant. Various types of arms were prohibited entirely, and the prime minister, acting through the governor in council, was given the power unilaterally to ban any firearm or other weapon he wishes.

As in the United Kingdom, Canadian legal authorities reject the idea of armed self-defense in any form and have used the gun laws to classify even small canisters of Mace, intended for self-defense, as prohibited weapons.

As a result of two new laws in the 1990s—one pushed by the Progressive Conservative government, the other by the succeeding Liberal government—approximately half of all registered handguns are to be confiscated without compensation upon the owner's death. A large number of shotguns and self-loading rifles have been banned or subjected to highly restrictive regulation. And all firearms must be registered with the police. The latter requirement is causing massive civil disobedience. The unpopular registration law has spurred the provincial governments of Alberta, Saskatchewan, and Manitoba to stop the administration and enforcement of all federal gun-control laws. Official estimates placed the cost of the new registration system at CA$85 (US$56) million. Independent estimates conservatively estimate the cost at CA$500 (US$330) million.

Criminals who want the control that firearms create readily circumvent firearms bans.

In addition, the Criminal Code prohibits "careless" storage of a firearm, and gives the government the authority to create storage regulations. Some incidents from 1996 and 1997 illustrate the practical effect of the law.

Hearing suspicious sounds, perhaps from a burglar, a husband took his unloaded rifle with him one night as he looked around his house. A few days later, the wife told a friend about the incident. Aghast, the friend called the police. The police arrived at the couple's home and bullied their way in. Searching the home, they found the unloaded rifle under a mattress in the bedroom. No children lived in the home. The couple was charged with careless storage of a firearm.

Another incident, involving a single woman who ran a small boarding house in Ontario, demonstrates the difficulty under restrictive regulations for a citizen to protect herself. A male downstairs tenant began harassing and stalking her. Worried that the woman might pose a threat to the tenant, the police searched her apartment and found several unloaded guns in her closets. She was convicted of storing a firearm in violation of regulations. She had been attending school and studying to become a paralegal, but her conviction bars her from a job in the legal field.

As David Tomlinson, President of Canada's National Firearms Association points out, safe storage laws are unenforceable without random police searches of the home. The new Liberal Party gun law, which was enacted in 1995, gives the police the authority to inspect private homes, without a warrant, to ensure that storage laws are being complied with.

Researchers differ about the efficacy of Canadian gun control. Some find that controls have led to increased crime against an ill-defended population. Notably, the Canadian Justice Department worked diligently with only partial success to suppress an independent research report, which had been commissioned by the Justice Department. The report showed the 1977 gun-owner licensing law had been a failure.

Problems down under

In contrast to Japan, the United Kingdom, and Canada, Australian gun laws are made at the state, not the national, level. In the 1920s and 30s, the eight Australian states enacted pistol and revolver registration. Long guns, including shotguns and rifles, remained lightly regulated, although controls began increasing in the 1980s.

Police licensing discretion is not always exercised reasonably. Politically connected individuals have been known to get handgun licenses without meeting the standard criteria, while in one major city the senior police officer unilaterally decided that no one except the police should have a firearm. And in New South Wales the police decided that only an approved steel safe bolted to the structure of the house constituted reasonable safe storage.

In April 1996, Australia's gun-control policy changed radically 12 days after a deranged gunman murdered 35 people in Port Arthur, Tasmania. At a May 10 meeting, the police ministers from the Australian states announced that all Australian governments had agreed to a 10-point plan for firearms regulation. All firearms were to be registered, and the sale, resale, transfer, ownership, possession, manufacture, and use of a variety of commonly owned firearms were banned. A buyback plan to compensate the owners of confiscated arms was announced at an estimated cost of AU$500 (US$275) million. Recreational shooters and hunters were required to get a series of licenses and permits. The only reasons for owning firearms were narrowed to permitted hunting, officially authorized vermin control, and participation in shooting sports such as those recognized by the International Olympic Committee. South Australia and Victoria still allow the arms used in paintball games, though South Australia requires their owners to obtain a license.

Though paintball—a game in which contestants shoot each other with harmless capsules of paint—is allowed, self-defense is not. Personal protection is not considered a justifiable reason to have a firearm in any jurisdiction. As far as the Australian governments were concerned, the actions of the murderer in Port Arthur had rendered Australians unfit to defend themselves against criminals. As in the United Kingdom, homeowners who use guns against violent home invaders are often charged with attempted murder.

In many ways, Australia's experiment with gun control is a solution in search of a problem. Even though an estimated one in five Australian households contained a gun before the 1996 legislation, Australia has always had relatively few problems with firearms. According to a 1995 report done for the Canadian Department of Justice, Australian homicide rates were very low by worldwide standards, and only 18 Australians died in accidents with firearms in 1993.

Evidence that surfaced after the legislative push indicated that Australian firearms control legislation had been ready for some time. Gun-control advocates, knowing that their utopian solution would be difficult to pass when people were unemotional about the subject, had been waiting until some horrific event created the requisite public hysteria.

In March 1997, Daryl Smeaton, the director of the Office of Law Enforcement Coordination, Commonwealth Attorney-General's Department, said that firearms control had been a regular item on the Australasian Police Ministers' Council agenda since 1981. In November 1995, the council resolved to release a working paper "as the basis for consultation with firearms interest groups." Promising the usual reductions in crime, suicide, and homicide, the substance of this working paper became law on May 10, 1996, a timetable that left no time for any substantial discussion.

By 1999, Inspector John McCoomb, the head of the Weapons Licensing Branch in Queensland, considered Australia's gun legislation a failure, saying that the gun ban had sent the weapons trade underground. Gangs and organized crime syndicates now run trade in firearms, and only a small fraction of the weapons in the country were turned in during the buyback.

Since restrictions deemed reasonable by the government have failed to eradicate crime, Australian authorities have resorted to the familiar pattern of extending government control to anything that could possibly be used as a weapon. As of May 1, 1998, New South Wales banned the sale of knives to anyone under 16. Possession is also illegal, a move that theoretically extends government control to children's hobbies since the ban included fishing knives, electric knives, and hobby knives. Victoria officials also planned to ban sales of knives to teenagers in early 2000. As part of the legislation, police would be armed with hand-held metal detectors while on patrol and would be given expanded powers to search for and confiscate knives.

The cost of gun control

Modern British, Canadian, Australian, and Japanese governments have now spent uncounted billions and many decades attempting to ban and restrict firearms. It has been a century of failure. Though banning firearms may reduce suicides and homicides committed with firearms, there is little evidence that a ban on firearms lowers the overall suicide or homicide rate. As defensive guns have been banned, overall violent crime rates have risen. People who want to kill themselves use another method, and criminals who want the control that firearms create readily circumvent firearms bans.

Moreover, prohibition has created a lucrative new criminal market in illegal weapons. Criminals by definition do not obey the law. Without firearms, most law-abiding citizens are no match even for unarmed criminals skilled in street fighting. Banning firearms reduces the risk and thus the cost to the perpetrator of crime. As basic economics would predict, when the cost falls, the supply rises.

As crime rises and illegal arms flood the country, governments react by making the possession of any weapon illegal, vastly expanding their powers of search and seizure and instituting zero-tolerance policies that make many ordinary activities illegal—such as carrying a knife to cut newspaper bundles or gut fish. Governments demonize anyone who argues that such policies go too far and often distort the meaning of official statistics in an effort to save face.

In short, gun control has corrupted the modern governments that have tried to institute it. Because gun control applies only to the law-abiding, governments who institute it deprive their productive citizens of the means to defend themselves effectively. Governments indirectly become the accomplice of murderers, rapists, and thugs.

5

Concealed-Carry Laws Deter Crime

John R. Lott Jr., interviewed by
Jacob Sullum and Michael W. Lynch

John R. Lott Jr. is a senior researcher at Yale University Law School and the author of More Guns, Less Crime. *The following viewpoint is adapted from an interview that Lott gave to the editors of* Reason *magazine.*

Studies show that allowing law-abiding citizens to carry concealed firearms reduces crime. Although the statistical methods used to prove this correlation are complex, the most likely explanation for why concealed-carry laws reduce crime is simple: Criminals are less likely to attack individuals who may be armed. In addition, "shall-issue" or " right-to-carry" laws, which require states to issue gun permits to everyone who meets certain criteria, are more effective in reducing crime than "may-issue" or "restrictive" laws, which give states more power to deny concealed-carry permits. Guns are used to stop crimes far more than mainstream media reports would indicate.

Until recently, when he bought a 9-mm Ruger after his own research impressed upon him the value of gun ownership, John Lott had no personal experience with firearms, aside from one day of riflery in summer camp when he was 12. That fact did not stop a reviewer of Lott's 1998 book, *More Guns, Less Crime*, from labeling him a "gun nut." Writing in *The American Prospect*, Edward Cohn also identified Lott as "a leading loon of the Chicago School of economics, known for its ultra-market ideology." But that was gentle—a backhanded compliment, even—compared to the attacks from anti-gun activists, who accused Lott of producing his landmark study at the behest of the gun industry.

Lott, now a senior research scholar at Yale Law School, used to be the John M. Olin Law and Economics Fellow at the University of Chicago. That position, like similar ones at other major universities, was endowed by a foundation based on the personal fortune of the late John M. Olin, former chairman of the Olin Corporation. Among many other things, the

Olin Corporation makes Winchester ammunition. These facts led Kristen Rand of the Violence Policy Center to conclude that "Lott's work was, in essence, funded by the firearms industry"—a charge that was echoed by other gun control advocates, including Charles Schumer, then a Democratic representative from New York and now a senator.

Never mind that assuming the Olin Foundation takes orders from "the firearms industry" is like assuming the Ford Foundation does the bidding of automakers. Never mind that Olin fellows are chosen by faculty committees, not by the foundation (with which Lott never had any contact). Proponents of gun control were desperate to discredit Lott, because his findings contradicted their dark predictions about what would happen if states allowed law-abiding citizens to carry concealed handguns.

Analyzing 18 years of data for more than 3,000 counties, Lott found that violent crime drops significantly when states switch from discretionary permit policies, which give local officials the authority to determine who may carry a gun, to "shall issue" or "right-to-carry" laws, which require that permits be granted to everyone who meets certain objective criteria. That conclusion, first set forth in a 1997 paper that Lott co-authored with David Mustard, now an economist at the University of Georgia, heartened defenders of gun ownership and dismayed their opponents. Arguing that "shall issue" laws are beneficial, while other gun laws are ineffective at best, Lott quickly became one of the most widely cited—and reviled—scholars in the gun control debate.

Though it was the gun issue that brought Lott notoriety, it hasn't been the focus of his career. The 41-year-old economist, who earned his Ph.D. at UCLA, has published papers on a wide variety of topics, including professional licensing, criminal punishment, campaign finance, and public education. Last summer he published *Are Predatory Commitments Credible?*, a skeptical look at theories of predatory pricing, and he is working on a book about the reputational penalties faced by criminals, a long-standing interest. In addition to his positions at Yale and the University of Chicago, Lott has served as chief economist at the U.S. Sentencing Commission and taught at UCLA and the University of Pennsylvania, among other schools. He lives in Swarthmore, Pennsylvania, with his wife and four children. [*Reason* magazine] Senior Editor Jacob Sullum and Washington Editor Michael Lynch talked to Lott at his Yale Law School office in mid-October [in 1999].

The research behind *More Guns, Less Crime*

Reason: *How did you become interested in guns?*

John R. Lott Jr.: About six years ago, I was teaching a class dealing with crime issues at the University of Pennsylvania, and it dawned on me that my students would be interested in some papers on gun control. It forced me to look at the literature systematically to decide what papers to assign to the class. I was shocked by how poorly done the existing research on guns and crime was.

You had very small samples. By far the largest previous study on guns and crime had looked at just 170 cities within a single year, 1980. Most of the rest looked at, say, 24 counties or 24 cities within a single year. No one had tried to account for things like arrest rates or conviction rates or prison sentence lengths. And the studies were all very limited in the sense that they were purely cross-sectional, where you look at the crime rates across jurisdictions in one year, or [purely longitudinal], where you pick one city or one county and look at it over time.

It was basically because of that class that I saw the benefit to going out and trying to do it right. So I put together what I think is by far the largest study that's ever been done on crime. The book has data on all 3,000-plus counties in the U.S. over an 18-year period. And simply having that large a data set allows you to account for hundreds of factors, thousands of factors, that you couldn't have accounted for in those smaller data sets. . . .

The thrust of your argument in More Guns, Less Crime *is easy enough to understand. But the details of the evidence you cite are hard to follow for anyone who is not trained in econometrics. Does it bother you that people who support the right to keep and bear arms are apt to accept your conclusions at face value, while those who are inclined to support gun control will tend to reject your findings, even though few people in either group are equipped to evaluate the evidence?*

Will allowing law-abiding citizens to carry concealed handguns save lives? The answer is yes, it will.

My guess is that [my critics] assume that the vast majority of people who hear their claims are not going to even look at the book. So they say, "Lott didn't account for poverty." Or they say, "Lott didn't account for other types of gun laws." Those are things that are easy to evaluate: Either I did, or I didn't. But I think they feel that they can get away with making those claims, because it'll be only a tiny fraction of 1 percent who will go and buy the book or get it from the library. I've never been involved in a debate like this, because in your normal academic debate, where there are 10 people involved and they've all read the paper, if somebody says, "Professor X didn't account for other gun laws," everybody else in the room would laugh, because they would know it was an absurd claim.

I don't think that most of the comments [the critics] are making are really that difficult to understand. One of the claims, for instance, is that I'm assuming that when these laws are passed there will be a one-time drop in violent crime rates, and it should be the same across all places that adopt these laws. That's absurd. I don't know how much time I spend in the book saying that the level of deterrence is related, according to the data, to the probability that people are going to be able to defend themselves, and the rate at which people get permits changes over time. When you pass these laws, not everybody who eventually is going to get a permit does it the first day. Fifteen years after these laws go into effect, you're still seeing an increasing percentage of the population getting these permits and a decreasing rate of violent crime because of the additional deterrence.

I spend lots of time in the book talking about why you don't expect the drop in crime to be the same in all places. . . .In more urban areas [of states with discretionary permit laws], public officials were especially reluctant to issue permits. So when you change to a nondiscretionary rule, the biggest increases in permits tended to be in these urban areas, and that is where you observe the biggest drops in violent crime.

Your analysis shows that liberal carry permit policies are associated with lower crime rates even after controlling for a variety of factors that might also have an impact on crime. In the book you concede that some other variable that you did not consider could be responsible for this association. Yet at the end of the book, you write, "Will allowing law-abiding citizens to carry concealed hand-guns save lives? The answer is yes, it will." Do statements like that go too far?

I don't think so. That's one of the last sentences in the book, and at that point the evidence is pretty overwhelming. There are different types of information, and they're all pointing in the same direction.

After these laws are adopted, you see a drop in violent crime, and it continues over time as the percentage of the population with permits increases. If I look at neighboring counties on either side of a state border, when one state passes its right-to-carry law, I see a drop in violent crime in that county, but the other county, right across the state border, in a state without a right-to-carry law, sees an increase in its violent crime rate. You try to control for differences in the legal system, arrest and conviction rates, different types of laws, demographics, poverty, drug prices—all sorts of things. You look at something like that, and I think it's pretty hard to come up with some other explanation. I think you're seeing some criminals move [across the state line].

You find the types of people who benefit the most from these laws. The biggest drops in crime are among women and the elderly, who are physically weaker, and in the high-crime, relatively poor areas where people are most vulnerable.

There are five or six things that one could point to that confirm different parts of the theory. I haven't heard anybody come up with a story that explains all these different pieces of evidence. . . . Since you have all these states changing their laws at different times, it becomes harder and harder to think of some left-out factor that just happened to be changing in all these different states at the same time the right-to-carry law got changed. . . .

A woman who behaves passively [when attacked] is 2.5 times as likely to end up being seriously injured as a woman who has a gun.

University of Florida criminologist Gary Kleck recently told The Salt Lake Tribune that "Lott has convincingly demonstrated there is no substantial detriment" from "shall issue" laws. But he questioned whether these laws could have as substantial a deterrent effect as you suggest. Kleck provided a blurb for your book, and his work is often cited by opponents of gun control. Why do you think he has trouble buying your conclusions?

Gary has had a strong opinion for a long time that, on net, guns neither reduce or increase crime. He thinks it's essentially a wash. And I'm not sure I understand how he comes to that conclusion, particularly given the survey data that indicate that many more violent crimes are stopped with guns than are perpetrated with guns. But it is something that he has written and felt strongly about for a long time. Now Gary may think that there's something else that's being left out that maybe could explain these changes in crime rates. If he can tell me what that factor is, I'd be happy to try to test it.

Do you still hear the argument that you're in the pay of the gun industry, or has that been discredited?

I think the gun control people are going to continue to bring it up. I've been in debates . . . with people from Handgun Control Inc. [now known as the Brady Campaign to Reduce Gun Violence] and other gun control groups in which they asserted flat-out that I've been paid by gun makers to do this study.

When they raise this charge, how successful are you in making the point that people should be able to assess evidence and arguments on their merits and that your motives don't matter?

Well, most people aren't going to look at the data. They're not going to have the data in front of them. The credibility of the data and the message depends on whether or not they believe that the person who's telling them about the data is credible. And I think the gun control groups feel that it's a win to the extent that they even divert three minutes of a show to talking about this issue. Even if it doesn't stick in people's minds, it's still three minutes that I couldn't talk about something else.

The effectiveness of defensive gun use

In a working paper you wrote with University of Chicago law professor William Landes, you conclude that "shall issue" laws are especially effective at preventing mass public shootings. Given that the people who commit these crimes seem to be pretty unbalanced, if not suicidal, how does the deterrent work?

Most of these attacks do end in the death of the attackers themselves, frequently from suicide, but also because they're killed by others. But part of what's motivating them is the desire to harm other people, and to the extent that you can take that away from them, I think you reduce their incentive to engage in these attacks. Whether they do it just because they intrinsically value killing people or whether they do it because of the publicity, the fact that there might be a citizen there who can stop them well before the police are able to arrive takes away, in their warped minds, some of the gain from the crime, and stops a lot of them from doing it. . . .

You say that resistance with a gun is the safest option when confronted by a criminal. What's the basis for that conclusion?

You hear claims from time to time that people should behave passively when they're confronted by a criminal. And if you push people on that, they'll refer to something called the National Crime Victimization Survey, a government project that surveys about 50,000 households each year. If you compare passive behavior to all forms of active resistance lumped together, passive behavior is indeed slightly safer than active resistance. But that's very misleading, because under the heading of active resistance you're lumping together things like using your fist, yelling and screaming, running away, using Mace, a baseball bat, a knife, or a gun. Some of those actions are indeed much more dangerous than passive behavior. But some are much safer.

For a woman, for example, by far the most dangerous course of action to take when she's confronted by a criminal is to use her fists. The reason is pretty simple: You're almost always talking about a male criminal doing the attacking, so in the case of a female victim there's a large strength differential. And for a woman to use her fists is very likely to result in a physical response from the attacker and a high probability of serious injury or death to the woman. For women, by far the safest course of action is to have a gun. A woman who behaves passively is 2.5 times as likely to end up being seriously injured as a woman who has a gun.

Why does the mainstream press seem to downplay the value of armed self-defense?

One question is, Why don't they report people using guns defensively? If I have two stories, one where there's a dead body on the ground vs. another where, say, a woman has brandished a gun and a would-be rapist or murderer has run away, with no shots fired and no dead body on the ground, it's pretty obvious to me which one of those is going to be considered more newsworthy. It doesn't require any conspiracy. Now if we care about policy, if we care about what types of actions are going to save the most lives, or prevent the most crimes, we want to look at both of those cases: not only the newsworthy bad events but the bad events that never become newsworthy because they don't occur.

But I don't think that explains everything. One example is gun deaths involving children. My guess is that if you go out and ask people, how many gun deaths involve children under age 5, or under age 10, in the United States, they're going to say thousands. When you tell them that in 1996 there were 17 gun deaths for children under age 5 in the United States and 44 for children under age 10, they're just astounded. There's a reason why they believe these deaths occur much more frequently: If you have a gun death in the home involving a child under age 5, you're going to get national news coverage. Five times more children drown in bathtubs; more than twice as many drown in five-gallon water buckets around the home. But those deaths do not get national news coverage.

This type of news coverage has consequences, because it affects people's perceptions of the benefits and costs of having guns around. Concentrating on gun deaths in the home, exaggerating the risks of that, creates a false impression. People are going to die because of that false impression. They're not going to have guns in the home, even though that's by far the safest course of action for them to take when they're confronted by a criminal. You may prevent some of the accidental deaths, but you're going to create other types of deaths because people won't be able to defend themselves.

I think the debate would be so different now if, even once in a while, some of the life-saving uses of guns got some attention in the news. A couple of the public school shootings were stopped by citizens armed with guns well before the police were able to arrive. Or take the case of the day trader shooting in Atlanta, which got huge attention. Within 10 days after that, there were three separate attacks in the Atlanta area that were stopped by citizens with guns, in two cases permitted concealed handguns. They got no attention outside of the local media market.

6

Concealed-Carry Laws May Increase Crime

Violence Policy Center

The Violence Policy Center is a gun control advocacy organization based in Washington, D.C.

In his book *More Guns, Less Crime*, John R. Lott Jr. cites Texas as an example of a state in which concealed-carry laws have effectively reduced crime. As a result, the National Rifle Association and other pro-gun groups are praising Texas's concealed-carry law as a model for other states. However, analysis of arrest records in Texas reveals that, contrary to gun activists' claims, "law-abiding citizens" are not the only people who have received gun permits in Texas. Thousands of Texans with concealed-carry permits have been arrested for rape, homicide, assault, drunk driving, and drug possession. These arrest data show that, instead of reducing crime, Texas's concealed-carry law has armed criminals and threatened public safety.

In 1995 the Texas legislature passed a "shall issue" concealed handgun law—creating a non-discretionary system under which state authorities *must* provide a concealed handgun license to any applicant who meets specific, objective criteria. Licenses issued under the new law became effective in January 1996.

To receive the standard four-year license, applicants must submit an application—with proficiency certificate, fingerprints, photographs, proof of age and residency, and a $140 fee—to the Texas Department of Public Safety (DPS). An additional fee is required for the mandatory 10 hours of firearms proficiency training. The DPS then has 60 days in which to conduct a background check on the applicant. At the end of the 60 days, the agency must either grant or deny the license. (The law stipulates, however, that the DPS may suspend the 60-day "mandatory issuance" period for up to 180 days if an additional background investigation is warranted.)

Unlike "shall issue" laws passed by other states, the Texas law is unique in that it requires law enforcement agencies to report certain incidents involving license holders to the Department of Public Safety. Under the law, such reports are required to be made only when a violation regarding illegal carrying or discharge of a firearm has occurred and only when the license holder has been arrested. In practice, a majority of arrests appear to be reported by law enforcement agencies to the licensing authority. Information about these incidents is limited, however, because of broad confidentiality provisions contained in the law.

As of September 1, 2001, public information about the arrests of Texas concealed handgun license holders became more limited than ever when a new state law took effect that redefined the record-keeping rules of the Texas Department of Public Safety. This new law authorized the DPS to "maintain statistics related to responses by law enforcement agencies on its website only in incidents in which persons licensed to carry concealed handguns are convicted of certain serious offenses."

Despite reporting obstacles and limitations, research conducted by the Violence Policy Center (VPC) reveals that many Texas license holders have been arrested for a wide range of crimes. Arrest data is regularly accepted as a valid measure of crime, reflecting law enforcement response to criminal activity. For example, arrest counts are used as a valid and reliable measure of law enforcement response to crime by the Federal Bureau of Investigation's (FBI) Uniform Crime Reporting Program. Regardless of whether or not an arrest involving a concealed handgun license holder results in a dismissal or conviction in court, each arrest reflects time and resources spent by law enforcement. In addition, arrest data for the general population of Texas aged 21 years and older is also made available by the Department of Public Safety, allowing for comparison of weapon-related arrests of concealed handgun license holders to the general population of Texas aged 21 years and older.

According to the Texas Department of Public Safety, Texas concealed handgun license holders were arrested for a total of 5,314 crimes from January 1, 1996, to August 31, 2001. Crimes for which license holders were arrested include: murder/attempted murder (including attempted murder of police officer), kidnapping, rape/sexual assault, assault, weapon-related offenses, drug-related offenses, burglary, and theft. . . .

"Shall issue" laws are too permissive

This [viewpoint] is [adapted from] the fourth version of *License to Kill*. In January 1998 the Violence Policy Center released its first study: *License to Kill: Arrests Involving Texas Concealed Handgun License Holders*. That study analyzed the DPS's concealed handgun license holder arrest data between January 1, 1996, and October 9, 1997, and found that concealed handgun license holders had been arrested for 946 crimes subsequent to licensure. In March 1999, a follow-up study, *License to Kill, and Kidnap, and Rape, and Drive Drunk*, analyzed arrest data between January 1, 1996, and December 31, 1998, and found that concealed handgun license holders had been arrested for more than 1,000 new crimes, for a total of 2,080 arrests. In August 2000, *License to Kill III: The Texas Concealed Handgun Law's Legacy of Crime and Violence* analyzed the data between January 1, 1996, and April 30, 2000, and found that Texas concealed handgun license holders had been arrested for nearly 1,300 additional crimes, for a total of 3,370 arrests. This edition is an update of the August 2000 report.

Supporters of "shall issue" concealed carry laws maintain that only "law-abiding citizens" apply for and receive concealed handgun licenses. At an April 18, 1996, press conference in Dallas, then–National Rifle Association (NRA) chief lobbyist Tanya Metaksa asserted, "As we get more information about right-to-carry, our point is made again and again. . . . People who get permits in states which have fair right-to-carry laws are law-abiding, upstanding community leaders who merely seek to exercise their right to self-defense." Clearly this is not the case. As shown in news articles and in the VPC's *License to Kill* studies, concealed handgun license holders are arrested for a multitude of offenses, including violent crimes such as murder, kidnapping, and sexual assault. Most concealed carry states keep information on the crimes committed by their concealed carry license holders hidden. This does not mean that crimes do not occur. As illustrated by the few states that have "shall issue" concealed carry and have had their concealed carry programs (however briefly) examined, concealed carry license holders are not the "upstanding community leaders" that pro-gun advocates promised. Allowing the public access to the information necessary to evaluate a concealed carry program is the minimum that a state should do when overseeing a program that involves the use of lethal force.

The NRA has made repeated statements to the press that its current Congressional agenda includes a national concealed carry law similar to the one in Texas. As conservative activist, NRA Board member, and NRA Life Member Grover Norquist [was quoted] in *Rolling Stone* magazine . . . :

> Over the next five to ten years, gun activists will press for a federal law allowing people to carry concealed weapons across state lines. Already, several dozen states have enacted concealed carry laws, but a nationwide law would be something else. 'If we get that, we've won,' says Norquist. 'It's over.'

More recently, at its annual meeting in April 2002, the NRA claimed that its efforts to expand concealed carry laws across the United States are on target. In a speech to members, NRA Executive Vice President Wayne LaPierre promised to capitalize on "increased momentum since [the September 11, 2001, terrorist attacks] for such laws.

Currently, there are 33 "shall issue" states and 11 "may issue" states. Additionally, there are six states which have no, or very limited, concealed carry: Illinois, Kansas, Missouri, Nebraska, Ohio, and Wisconsin. In recent years, the Midwest states have been a battleground for the concealed carry issue. In a decisive defeat of NRA money, Missouri voters rejected concealed carry in a statewide referendum in 1998.

Arrests of gun owners

[There were] 5,314 arrests of these "law-abiding" concealed handgun license holders subsequent to licensure, as reported to the Texas DPS. Incidents involving concealed handgun license holders include: 41 arrests for murder or attempted murder, 14 arrests for kidnapping/false imprisonment, 79 arrests for rape/sexual assault, 279 arrests for alleged assault/

aggravated assault with a deadly weapon, 1,315 arrests for driving while intoxicated, 60 arrests for indecency with children, 404 drug-related arrests, 134 individual arrests for sexual misconduct, 19 arrests for impersonating a police officer or public servant, and eight arrests for arson.

VPC analysis of the DPS information reveals that—

- Texas concealed handgun license holders have been arrested for *two and one-half crimes a day* since the law went into effect.
- Texas concealed handgun license holders have been arrested for *more than two serious violent crimes per month* since the law went into effect, including: murder/attempted murder, manslaughter/negligent homicide, kidnapping, rape, and sexual assault.
- Texas concealed handgun license holders have been arrested for *more than two crimes against children per month* since the law went into effect, including: sexual assault/aggravated sexual assault on a child, injury to a child, indecency with a child, abandon/endanger a child, solicitation of a minor, and possession or promotion of child pornography.
- Texas concealed handgun license holders have been arrested for *more than four drunk driving offenses per week* since the law went into effect.
- Family violence was identified in *one in 23 incidents* involving concealed handgun license holders.
- Texas concealed handgun license holders have been arrested for *more than one weapon-related offense every other day* since the law went into effect.
- From 1996 to 2000, Texas concealed handgun license holders were arrested for weapon-related offenses *at a rate 81 percent higher than that of the general population of Texas, aged 21 and older.* These weapon-related offenses include arrests for 279 assaults or aggravated assaults with a deadly weapon, 671 unlawfully carrying a weapon, and 172 deadly conduct/discharge firearm. . . .

While advocates of relaxed concealed carry laws promise the public protection from crime, Texas Department of Public Safety data details the day-to-day, real-world effect of such laws: they arm criminals and threaten public safety. All too often, concealed carry license holders don't stop crimes, but commit them.

Yet, exactly how many and what types of crimes are being committed is becoming harder to ascertain. Texas, which allows information about the arrests of the concealed handgun license holders to be analyzed by the public, has taken the first step toward restricting information with the enactment of legislation, which took effect September 2001, restricting information posted on the Department of Public Safety's web site. Other states do not provide any information *at all* about the number and types of crimes committed by their concealed carry licensees. Allowing the public full access to this information on concealed carry holders is essential to a fair examination of the concealed carry licensing system.

In light of the findings of this study, and previous studies conducted by the Violence Policy Center of the Texas as well as Florida concealed carry laws, the VPC strongly recommends against the adoption of concealed carry licensing in any additional states and urges states that have passed such laws to repeal them.

7

Gun Licensing and Registration Would Reduce Crime

Brady Campaign to Prevent Gun Violence

The Brady Campaign to Prevent Gun Violence, formerly called Handgun Control, Inc., is a gun control advocacy organization based in Washington, D.C.

In order to reduce gun crime and violence, the United States needs a more effective national system of gun licensing and registration. Effective gun licensing would require potential gun purchasers to undergo a comprehensive background check and to complete a firearm safety course before a gun could be purchased. Effective gun registration would entail the creation of a national database in which the serial number of every handgun is recorded. This information would enable law enforcement to trace a gun used in a crime to its owner and to the person who sold the gun. For licensing and registration to be most effective, the government must also regulate secondary or private gun sales, such as those at gun shows, that currently are not subject to mandatory background checks.

Why does America need handgun licensing and registration?
In order to stem the flow of handgun violence, America needs a national system of handgun owner licensing. Handguns should be treated like cars in that owners would be licensed and handguns would be registered. Congress would establish minimum standards for the licensing system, which would be implemented by the states. Without a national system, gun traffickers will continue to make mass purchases of handguns in states with weak laws and sell them into the illegal market across the country. Minimum national standards will help to stop interstate gun trafficking and ensure that everyone who buys a handgun in this country is qualified to own one.

Licensing and registration—on a nationwide basis—are needed to curb the trafficking in guns that is responsible for the easy availability of guns on the streets of our nation.

Licensing and registration will also provide law enforcement with the means to prevent individuals like Mark Barton (the day-trader who shot and killed 12 people in Atlanta, Georgia in 1999) and Buford Furrow (the neo-Nazi who killed a Filipino postman and shot 5 people at a Jewish day-care center in Los Angeles, California in 1999) from obtaining guns. Both of these individuals had been diagnosed as mentally disturbed and dangerous. Had a licensing and registration system been in place, the police would have known if they possessed any firearms already and their licenses could have been revoked, preventing them from buying any other firearms. State licensing and registration requirements are already valuable law enforcement tools in the states where they exist and serve to reduce gun violence, but the effectiveness of existing laws is undermined by the lack of a national policy.

Licensing gun owners

What would a state licensing system entail?

Applicants would apply for their licenses with a state-authorized entity. Upon successful completion of the process, licensees would be issued a simple permit or a card, similar to a driver's license, which contains a picture ID and other identifying data, including address and date-of-birth. The license may be generally applicable to their specific weapon. Ideally, licenses would be issued for a limited period (e.g., 2 years) and require a background check upon renewal to make sure that the licensee has not committed any crimes since last renewing his/her license.

Why is licensing important?

Handgun licenses are necessary to stem the flow of guns into the wrong hands. No one who is prohibited by law from purchasing or owning a firearm should have one. By the same token, licensing would not affect the ability of law-abiding citizens to own or buy guns.

Licensing offers advantages over a simple waiting period/background check requirement and, most important, it should be required for any sale or transfer of a handgun. The process would keep handguns out of the wrong hands in the first place, without affecting the ability of a law-abiding citizen to buy firearms.

Various elements of the licensing system are all designed to prevent unauthorized and illegal access to handguns. For example, a more thorough background check, including fingerprint identification, would stop felons from acquiring guns through use of a false identification. Residency verification would preclude buyers and gunrunners from going to another state to take advantage of weaker gun laws. Finally, successful completion of a safety training course would ensure that gun owners are familiar with the safe handling of their weapons and with all relevant gun laws, and it would educate them on the risks posed by possession of handguns.

Licenses should be issued by the local law enforcement authority, such as the police chief or sheriff, and the process must provide an adequate length of time to conduct a thorough examination of the applicant's background. Before taking possession of a handgun, a person should have to display their license and the dealer should ascertain its validity by conducting a check with the state or local police. A three-day waiting period should be required before the actual transfer takes place.

What is the difference between licensing and registration?

Handgun licenses are issued to individuals and entitle the holder to purchase, receive or possess a handgun or firearm. Registration is a record of the transfer or ownership of a specific handgun.

Firearm registration

How do registration laws work?

Registration and record of sales laws apply to a specific handgun or firearm. Registration in its strictest form places the burden on the owners of firearms to register their weapons, usually by serial number and description, with a governmental authority, either local or state police.

Record of sales laws put a duty on a licensed firearms dealer to record information about the purchaser and firearm. The record can either be retained by the dealer or forwarded to an appropriate governmental authority. This system is usually limited to the registering of handgun or firearm transfers. Under this more limited approach, handguns or firearms are registered only when they are sold or otherwise transferred. Information on the sale or transfer, including the name and address of the purchaser, is sent to local or state police by the dealer, not the owner.

The [licensing] process would keep handguns out of the wrong hands in the first place, without affecting the ability of a law-abiding citizen to buy firearms.

What is the purpose of registration?

Registration allows for speedier and more reliable tracing of guns used in crime. Without registration, local or state officials must go to the Bureau of Alcohol, Tobacco and Firearms (BATF) for assistance in tracing guns. BATF, in turn, contacts the manufacturer of the gun, who in turn identifies the Federal Firearms Licensee (FFL) to whom the gun was sold. BATF must then seek the cooperation of the FFL in determining who bought the gun from the FFL. If subsequent, or secondary, transfers are not recorded, the investigation can quickly lead to a dead end. An untold number of criminals escape conviction because there is no paper trail or evidence linking them to the crime guns they used.

Registration is designed to reduce illegal gun trafficking by providing for more efficient tracing of guns used in crimes and tougher prosecution of those who sell guns to illegal purchasers. State-based registration of handgun transfers can achieve that objective.

States with licensing laws

Fourteen states have some elements of handgun owner licensing—though these systems vary greatly in their requirements, ranging from a formal licensing system similar to drivers' licenses to simply requiring a handgun safety course: California, Connecticut, Hawaii, Illinois, Iowa, Massachusetts, Michigan, Minnesota, Missouri, Nebraska, New Jersey, New York, North Carolina and Rhode Island.

What does licensing and registration entail?

Under the proposed system, any person would have to obtain a license in order to purchase or receive any handgun or handgun ammunition. In many ways, it would be like a driver's license and would be issued by states. Licenses (or permits to purchase, as they are often called) would be issued by state governments for purposes of regulating the sale, transfer or possession of handguns.

Registration is necessary to trace the flow of guns. Every firearm already has a serial number; however, there is no easy way to trace guns to purchasers, especially when guns are bought and sold privately. Without registration, guns flow easily from legal sales into the illegal market. Americans register their cars; they can easily register their handguns.

What are some of the proposed regulations?

Currently, licensing requirements vary between states. The proposed system for an applicant to receive a license would include:

1. Minimum age of 21. Currently, federal law prohibits federally licensed firearms dealers from selling handguns to persons under 21. However, a loophole in federal law allows the private sale of handguns to persons between the ages of 18 and 20. Only 12 states prohibit such sales to juveniles. Most states do not even require a background check for private sales to people under 21.

2. *Background check with fingerprint identification.* A name-based criminal history background check must be complemented with a fingerprint check. An FBI fingerprint background check provides the most reliable proof of identity and will ensure that felons and other prohibited persons are denied licenses.

3. *Proof of residency.* It is illegal to purchase a handgun outside the purchaser's state of residence. In addition to providing a driver's license, the applicant should be required to provide concrete proof of current residence such as a utility bill.

4. *Successful completion of a firearms safety test or course.* Currently only six states require any type of training or safety test before the purchase of a handgun. An untrained handgun owner is a danger to themselves, their family and the community, and should be required to demonstrate that he can load, fire and store a weapon safely. Training would also include education on federal, state and local laws related to gun ownership and use. Just as drivers must show they know the rules of the road, so should gun owners show that they are familiar with basic gun laws.

Which states have registration laws?

Hawaii and the District of Columbia provide for the registration of handguns or firearms. Twenty-one states have record-of-sales laws: Alabama; Alaska; California; Colorado; Connecticut; Delaware; Illinois; Indiana; Maryland; Massachusetts; Michigan; Minnesota; New Hampshire; New Jersey; New York; North Carolina; Pennsylvania; Rhode Island; Vermont; Washington; and Wyoming.

Note: Record-of-sales laws vary dramatically. Several—like California, Maryland, Massachusetts and Minnesota—require information on gun sales to be for-

warded to a state authority for centralized tracking. Others merely require local law enforcement to retain the information, usually for a limited period of time. . . .

Background checks on all handgun sales

What are "secondary" or "private" gun sales?

Gun purchases from licensed dealers are known as "primary" or "initial" purchases, and such purchases are subject to the federal Brady Criminal Background Check. A "secondary" or "private" gun sale is the reselling of a gun by a private individual (not a licensed gun dealer). Secondary or private sales are not subject to the federal Brady Criminal Background Check and are often not regulated by state law either. Secondary or private sales that avoid the background check, such as may occur at gun shows or over the internet, represent a dangerous loophole in the background check system.

Why require background checks on all handgun purchases?

When an individual buys a handgun from a licensed dealer, there are generally state and federal requirements for a background check to ensure that the purchaser is not prohibited from purchasing or possessing a firearm. However, in many states, when an individual wants to buy a handgun from another private citizen who is not a licensed gun dealer, there is no requirement to ensure that the purchaser is not in a prohibited category. This creates a huge loophole, which makes it easy for criminals, mentally ill persons, juveniles and others to evade background checks and buy guns. This loophole is the gateway to the illegal market. Obviously, the secondary or private sales market is attractive to criminals because they are not subject to a background check and no record is made of the sale. The Brady Campaign advocates closing this major loophole by requiring a background check on all handgun sales, including those by individuals, guns sold by unlicensed sellers at gun shows, and guns sold over the internet and through newspaper advertisements.

Registration allows for speedier and more reliable tracing of guns used in crime.

Why are private handgun sales a concern?

Unregulated, private or secondary handgun sales create opportunities for criminals and other prohibited purchasers to obtain guns. Criminals, knowing that they will face a background check at a licensed gun dealer, consistently buy guns from the secondary sales market to evade the background check requirement. Criminals also use individuals willing to purchase firearms for them, known as "straw purchasers." These people are not legally prohibited from buying a firearm and can purchase guns from licensed dealers and then resell them in secondary/private sales to criminals and gang members.

Requiring background checks and registration of both primary sales (sales by a licensed firearm dealer) and secondary sales puts straw purchasers and illegal gun dealers at risk of criminal prosecution. Gun owners who knowingly sell their guns to criminals or other disqualified buyers could be held criminally liable if the gun is later used in the commission of a crime.

The following examples clearly illustrate why secondary sales are a problem for law enforcement and the community at large:

• On October 10, 1997, George "Ezra" Edward Petersen used a Norinco MAK-90 to shoot and kill Captain Chris McCurley of the Etowah County (AL) Sheriff's Department during the execution of a drug search warrant at Petersen's home. Petersen had gotten his assault weapon from Ricky Lynn Smith, who was later convicted of selling the rifle to Petersen, a man Smith knew to be a convicted felon.

• On April 20, 1999, Columbine High School students Dylan Klebold and Erik Harris shot and killed 12 classmates and a teacher, wounding several others. In addition to a rifle and two shotguns, Klebold and Harris used a TEC-DC9 assault pistol to carry out their rampage.

The Brady Campaign advocates . . . requiring a background check on all handgun sales, including those by individuals.

The shooters were both under the age of 18 at the time of the shooting and therefore not legally able to buy the weapons themselves. However, their friend Robyn Anderson, who was over 18, purchased the shotguns and rifle for them at a gun show. Mark Manes, 22, sold them the assault pistol and later pled guilty to supplying a handgun to a minor.

• In March of 2000, Joseph C. Palczynski abducted his ex-girlfriend and killed four people in a two-week standoff with authorities in Maryland. Palczynski was armed with an AR-15 assault rifle and a Mossberg shotgun.

Palczynski was unable to purchase the weapons from a licensed dealer because he had a history of mental problems and had been convicted of assault. However, he drove his neighbor Constance A. Waugh to two gun shops on March 6 and gave her cash to purchase a 12-gauge shotgun and an AR-15 assault rifle for him, telling her he wanted to engage in target practice. Waugh later pled guilty to knowingly providing firearms to a convicted felon. Brian Chagnon, the son of two of Palczynski's victims said, "Her direct actions caused a lot of harm in a lot of people's lives."

• On September 17, 2001, Marion County (IN) sheriff's deputy Jason Baker was killed in a shootout with convicted felon Allen Dumperth and Michael Shannon after the men fled from a routine traffic stop. Dumperth and Shannon were armed with an SKS assault rifle and an AK-47 assault rifle.

The guns were supplied by straw purchaser Joshua Meadows, who bought both guns legally at Indianapolis gun stores earlier that year. Meadows was later convicted of supplying the weapons to Dumperth, knowing that he was a felon. "Joshua Meadows wasn't there that night. But he's the guy who toppled the first dominoes," said the slain deputy's father.

Why do private handgun sales need to be regulated?

Regulating private handgun sales will help to stop the flow of guns onto the black market. Cracking down on the illegal gun trafficking market is critical to reducing gun death and injuries. Every year, handguns are transferred from person to person with no background check and no record of the transaction. There is no accountability regarding sales to prohibited purchasers.

The illegal market exists for a variety of reasons. Criminals are unable to buy handguns from licensed dealers, because licensed dealers are required to conduct background checks on prospective gun buyers. Those background checks will detect a criminal's record and disqualify him or her from buying a gun. So these criminals turn to the unregulated secondary market. People who may not have a criminal record as yet, but intend to commit crimes, also turn to the secondary sales market because they want to make it difficult for law enforcement to trace a gun back to them.

Project Lead, a study conducted by the Bureau of Alcohol, Tobacco and Firearms, traced 2,465 firearms used in crime in Maryland from 1993 through 1995. Only 60 of these were found in the possession of the original purchaser. Therefore, the secondary sales market accounted for placing 2,405 guns into the hands of criminals in Maryland during that time period. In 1996, Maryland passed a law that extends the state's seven-day waiting period and background check to private sales.

How do states regulate private handgun sales?

Seventeen states regulate private sales in some manner, from licensing handgun buyers to requiring background checks on all sales at gun shows (gun shows are a primary secondary sales marketplace). Those states are California, Colorado, Connecticut, Hawaii, Illinois, Iowa, Maryland, Massachusetts, Michigan, Missouri, Nebraska, New Jersey, New York, North Carolina, Oregon, Pennsylvania, and Rhode Island.

Regulating private handgun sales will help to stop the flow of guns onto the black market.

Maryland: A Good Example of Why These Laws Are Enacted and How They Work. Prior to enacting its secondary sales law in Maryland in 1996, the Governor's Commission on Gun Violence found that secondary sales of firearms were at least equal to the annual number of firearms sold by licensed firearms dealers. This means that, in Maryland, half of the firearms sales were done with no background check and no record of the transaction. There is no way of knowing how many criminals received guns through these sales. The following further illustrate the need for secondary sales laws in that state:

- The Maryland State Police found that, of the firearms recovered in 1996, only 5% were seized from the individual recorded as the original purchaser. This means that 95% of these "crime guns" were acquired by the criminal through the secondary sales market.
- The 1994 Baltimore Trace Study demonstrates that 1,303 of the firearms confiscated between April 1, 1993 and March 31, 1994 were at least 7 to 8 years old. These guns could have gone through several changes in ownership during that time period, with no record of the owners along the way.
- Federal and state law enforcement officials, who were actively involved in passing laws in Maryland, testified before the Governor's

Commission on Gun Violence (Maryland) stating that straw purchasers and secondary sales were a major problem in controlling gun violence.

Examples of Other States That Regulate Private Sales.
- In Pennsylvania, legislation regulating private sales passed in 1995, as part of a comprehensive firearms bill that even had the support of the National Rifle Association. The NRA broke new ground with its support for this proposal, which they have vehemently opposed in other states. Now, in Pennsylvania, any individual who wants to sell his or her handgun has to get a background check on the purchaser. Seller liability—both criminal and civil—applies to the purchaser. The sale must be completed at a licensed dealer or in the sheriff's office to allow for the background check.
- In New Jersey, only persons with a "Permit to Purchase" can legally obtain a handgun, either from licensed dealers or individuals. The "Permit to Purchase" is issued by the applicant's police chief after a 30-day waiting period in which an in-depth background check is completed. Fingerprints are required from first time applicants. The seller must forward copies of the permit, which are valid for 90 days, to the police chief and the State Police.
- In California, all gun transfers must be processed through either a licensed gun dealer or law enforcement and are subject to a 10-day waiting period and background check. California handgun buyers must first obtain a state safety certificate as well.

Does the public support private handgun sales laws?

The 1999 National Gun Policy Survey, conducted by the National Opinion Research Center at the University of Chicago, found that 80% of those surveyed favor mandatory registration of handguns and 79% favor background checks on private sales of handguns, just as background checks are conducted on sales by licensed dealers.

Regulating secondary sales will not prevent law-abiding citizens from buying a gun from a friend or relative. Instead, it would curb the number of criminals who purchase guns by creating a level of accountability in the transfer of the firearm.

Why do states need to regulate private handgun sales?

Regulating the private sales of handguns is a sensible method of augmenting current federal and state laws, which cover the primary legal sale of a handgun. Since handguns tend to change ownership throughout their existence, it only makes sense that the changes in ownership along the way should be conducted in the same careful manner as the first sale from a licensed firearms dealer.

Allowing secondary handgun sales to go unregulated will continue to feed the supply of guns to criminals and other prohibited buyers, causing needless injury and loss of life. A way to assist law enforcement, and the communities which will continue to be adversely affected by this problem, is to enact state legislation regulating the selling and giving of handguns between private parties.

8

Gun Licensing and Registration Would Not Reduce Crime

James B. Jacobs

James B. Jacobs is a professor of law at New York University and the author of Can Gun Control Work? *from which the following viewpoint is excerpted.*

In 1993 the federal government enacted the Brady Law, which mandates a five-day waiting period for gun purchases, during which a background check is run on prospective gun buyers. However, the law only applies to Federal Firearms Licensees (FFLs), and not to unlicensed or individual sellers who deal in the secondary market. Since the passage of the Brady Bill, gun control advocates have been touting another bill known as "Brady II" that seeks to institute a more comprehensive national system of licensing gun owners and tracking all gun purchases. However, Brady II's proposed licensing and registration system would do little to impact the vast black market in firearms, through which criminals would still be able to obtain guns. Even among normally law-abiding gun owners, there would be resistance to gun licensing and registration that would make the system ultimately ineffective.

Just after the Brady Bill became law, handgun control advocates began pushing a new omnibus gun control bill that would create a comprehensive handgun licensing and registration system. In effect, the proponents of the new bill (popularly called "Brady II") claimed, at one and the same time, that the 1993 Brady Law was a giant step toward reducing gun crime and merely a small step toward that goal.[1] By means of licensing and registration, "Brady II" seeks to extend the Brady Law to the secondary market of handgun transfers between nondealers. Brady II (Gun Violence Prevention Act of 1994) requires states to enact handgun licens-

1. The Brady II bill had not been passed into law at the time this volume went to press.

ing laws meeting minimum federal standards. It also requires that handguns be registered in order to be transferred, thereby establishing a national handgun registry, albeit one that would take decades to mature. . . .

Universal handgun licensing

Brady II significantly extends Brady I by making it illegal "for any person to sell, deliver, or otherwise transfer a handgun to an individual who is not [a Federal Firearms Licensee] unless the transferor verifies that the transferee possesses a valid state handgun license." It makes it unlawful for anyone, other than an FFL, to receive a handgun or handgun ammunition "unless the individual possesses a valid state handgun license." By contrast, currently only 11 states require a permit for handgun purchases. The proposed law would prohibit not only handgun sales by an FFL to an unlicensed purchaser but also sales in the secondary market by a nondealer to an unlicensed individual. It would also prohibit gifts and loans of handguns to unlicensed individuals. . . .

Evading the Brady II licensing system

A person ineligible for a handgun license could try to evade the Brady II licensing system by persuading a gun owner to sell or "lend" him a handgun, or he could use a counterfeit, stolen, or borrowed handgun license. We can anticipate that if licenses became necessary to purchase handguns from FFLs, counterfeit licenses would become available on the black market, just as fake drivers licenses and other identification documents are now available. A fake license would be especially effective in duping an unsophisticated gun seller. Furthermore, an unlicensed person could use a licensed straw purchaser to buy a handgun on his behalf. Of course, unlicensed persons could also steal handguns.

Under the Brady II regulatory regime, a handgun transfer to an unlicensed purchaser would not set off any warning bells. As long as the unlicensed purchaser is not caught with the handgun, the unlawful sale would go unnoticed. There would probably be less risk of an unlicensed gun owner being caught than an unlicensed driver. In testimony before Congress, Jo Ann Harris, assistant attorney general, Criminal Division, U.S. Department of Justice, explained the difficulty of apprehending felons who unlawfully possess guns, despite it being a federal crime punishable by up to 10 years in prison.

> The most common way we come across a 922(g) [felon-in-possession] violation is when the person has committed another crime. It is difficult for law enforcement to learn about and be able to prosecute a 922(g) without their having committed another crime because it is very difficult to find them in possession.

Because Brady II only requires a handgun owner to obtain a license before taking possession of a *new* gun, a person arrested for possession of a handgun without a license might escape punishment by falsely claiming that he did not need a license because he owned this handgun before Brady II went into effect. How could that claim be disproved? (Of course, if the handgun had been manufactured subsequent to passage of Brady II, that story would not fly.)

Even if he admitted obtaining the handgun after Brady II became effective, federal prosecutors will almost certainly lack the resources or inclination to bring prosecutions against every otherwise law-abiding individual who fails to comply with Brady II's licensing requirements. Consider that, currently, federal prosecutors do not eagerly accept for prosecution even *felon-in-possession* (so-called 922[g]) cases, unless the felon is a hardened criminal. According to Assistant Attorney General Jo Ann Harris, prosecuting every felon-in-possession case would "not be good law enforcement policy." Furthermore, a study of cases presented to the U.S. Attorney's Office for the Northern District of Illinois found that only 24% of prosecutable weapons and explosives offenses were actually prosecuted. In 47% of weapons cases declined for prosecution, the screening prosecutor's reason was that the case involved a "minor offense." In 1993, U.S. attorneys' offices nationwide declined to prosecute 27.6% of weapons offenses. Unfortunately for the prosecution, jurors, especially in southern and western states, may be unwilling to convict a defendant whose only crime is unlicensed possession of a handgun.

An unlicensed person could use a licensed straw purchaser to buy a handgun on his behalf.

If the unlawful handgun transfer did come to light, the transferor (assuming he could be traced and found) might falsely claim that he never sold, lent, or gave the gun to anybody; to the contrary, he did not realize the gun was missing. Brady II requires that within 24 hours after discovering that a handgun has been stolen or lost, the licensee must report the theft or loss to the secretary of the treasury, the CLEO [state's chief law enforcement officer], and local law enforcement. Failure to do so is punishable by a civil penalty of not less than $1,000. Still, the gun owner may argue that because he completely lacks knowledge that the gun had been stolen, he ought to be absolved of any liability, criminal or civil. Another story the transferor may tell is that the person to whom he transferred the handgun did appear to have a valid license and that he did fill out and file all the relevant forms: in other words, he could falsely claim to be the victim of the gun recipient's fraud or a bureaucratic blunder.

Would Brady II make it significantly more difficult for criminals to obtain a handgun? Probably not. First, many criminals already own a handgun or have ready access to one through a friend, family member, or gang associate. Second, many criminals obtain guns by theft or by informal transfers from other criminals, especially drug dealers and addicts. Criminals who are not deterred by existing criminal laws, prohibiting the conduct they regularly engage in, are unlikely to worry about illegally selling or transferring a handgun.

Brady II's registration system

Under existing law, manufacturers must engrave a serial number on the barrel of each handgun. Manufacturers, wholesalers, and dealers must maintain records of each handgun sale (including serial number, make, model, and the name and address of the purchaser) and supply such information to the secretary of the treasury upon request, in the course of a bona fide BATF [Bureau of Alcohol, Tobacco, and Firearms] or law enforcement investigation. As things now stand, if the FFL maintains records in the manner prescribed by law, if the police find a gun with its serial number intact, it can be traced to its first retail purchaser. After that, there is no paper record of a gun's chain of ownership. That is where Brady II would come in by establishing a comprehensive handgun registration system. This is a completely new policy initiative. Other than the National Firearms Registration and Transfer Record (NFRTR) system for machine guns that has existed since 1934, the federal government has never tried to maintain a firearms registry. . . .

Nowhere in Brady II do we find the words *national handgun registry*, but this is what the bill would establish. Brady II would expand the paper trail on every handgun by requiring the manufacturer and all subsequent sellers or transferors (after verifying the prospective buyer's handgun license and eligibility) to fill out a registration form that includes the purchaser's name and address, handgun license number, and information about the handgun, including make, model, and serial number. . . .

Would Brady II make it significantly more difficult for criminals to obtain a handgun? Probably not.

The goal would be to achieve an easily accessible ownership record for every handgun in the United States. Since many owners would not sell their handguns for years, perhaps decades, it would take a long time for the registry to become complete. But, in theory, when fully mature, the system would look like the registration systems we now have for houses and automobiles, except that Brady II would establish a national registry, not fifty separate state-based systems.

Goal of the handgun registration system

A national registry would play a crucial role in supporting the handgun licensing system. Indeed, without a record of a gun's ownership, it would be difficult to prove that a particular individual had sold a specific handgun to a particular person. Without comprehensive registration, many sellers might feel that they could with impunity ignore the duty to sell handguns only to licensed persons. Registration is a strategy for deterring licensed owners from selling handguns to people who are ineligible to possess them.

Suppose the police arrest a criminal suspect who is found to have a handgun manufactured after the effective date of Brady II. If the suspect does not have a handgun license, he must have obtained this handgun illegally, but from whom—an unscrupulous FFL? A casual arm's length seller? A black market gun dealer? A drug dealer? A criminal comrade? A friend or relative? Without that handgun's history, there would be no way (other than the suspect's testimony) to figure out who sold or gave the handgun to the criminal suspect. In theory, registration provides the paper trail enabling the police to identify the handgun's last owner. Investigators could confront the last registered owner, demanding to know how it is that a handgun registered to him is now in the hands of a criminal; there is no record of the handgun having been transferred or any record of the handgun having been reported as stolen or lost.

The biggest impediment to implementing a national handgun registry is obtaining compliance from handgun owners.

Would a national handgun registry help prevent or solve crime? Suppose the police could send the serial number of a gun recovered at a crime scene to the proposed National Tracing Center, which could immediately identify the registered owner. The police would then have a suspect.

This crime-solving potential is diminished by a few realities. If the gun is recovered at the scene, it is usually because the police have arrested the person holding it. In the overwhelming majority of crimes, where an offender successfully flees the scene of the crime, the gun is never recovered.

A savvy criminal could defeat the tracing system by obliterating the serial number with a file or some other tool. Currently, an estimated 20% of guns submitted to the BATF are untraceable for this reason. [Researchers] Sheley and Wright reported that their juvenile inmate respondents listed firepower, quality of construction, and untraceability as the three most desirable qualities for a gun. It remains to be seen whether the secretary of the treasury could come up with a foolproof scheme for marking guns with unremovable serial numbers. Perhaps new technology, such as a computer chip containing a serial number, could prevent destruction of a gun's identity. Of course, handguns manufactured before the new technology came on line would still be vulnerable to obliteration of the serial number and would continue to be untraceable.

BATF's National Firearms Tracing Center has been used mostly for gathering intelligence about the origins and interstate migration of crime guns, not for solving individual gun crimes. At best, tracing identifies the manufacturers and FFLs whose guns are disproportionately used in crime. This goal could be achieved without expanding the current regulatory system. Under existing laws and regulations, unless the serial number has been obliterated, a firearm can be traced back to its manufacturer and from the manufacturer to the wholesaler, then to the FFL retailer, and finally to the first purchaser.

Handguns move from the legitimate market into the hands of criminals through thefts, purchases in the secondary market, loans and gifts from family members, friends, and criminal comrades. Some corrupt FFLs specialize in selling handguns to criminals or to traffickers who, in turn, sell them to criminals. The BATF reported that in 1996, about 60% of successfully traced crime guns originated with 1% of all FFLs. The current tracing system can identify corrupt FFLs. It is hard to see how Brady II would significantly improve the investigation of black marketeers and gun runners.

Evading the registration system

The biggest impediment to implementing a national handgun registry is obtaining compliance from handgun owners. There is no doubt that any gun registration system would be met by massive resistance because of the fear that registration would lead the way to confiscation. Tanya K. Metaksa, the former director of the NRA's [National Rifle Association's] Institute for Legislative Action, has articulated an attitude toward registration that is likely to be widely shared.

> Time after time, firearms registration systems have led inexorably toward firearms confiscation. The lessons of history are vivid in the minds of gun owners who value their rights. From gun confiscation schemes launched by the former Soviet Union against Lithuania to turn-guns-in-or-go-to-jail policies in California, gun lists become gun losses, and gun owners know it.

Given many gun owners' hostility to registration and their belief that a registration system would later be used to confiscate all handguns (as occurred in Britain), there would certainly be significant noncompliance. Indeed, if a current handgun owner decided to sell and wanted to avoid the registration requirement, he could easily find a buyer of like mind, and so on down the line. A single handgun could be sold again and again without being registered and with little risk of detection.

Enforcing a licensing scheme in the secondary market would require a herculean enforcement effort.

In recent years, several states and municipalities passed laws mandating the registration of assault rifles. These laws were overwhelmingly ignored. In Boston and Cleveland, the rate of compliance with bans on assault rifles is estimated at 1%. Out of the 100,000 to 300,000 assault rifles estimated to be in private hands in New Jersey, 947 were registered, an additional 888 rendered inoperable, and 4 turned over to the authorities. In California, nearly 90% of the approximately 300,000 assault weapons owners did not register their weapons.

Even if a significant percentage of law-abiding handgun owners complied with the registration law, we can be certain that *handgun-owning criminals would not comply*, because in so doing they would be admitting to felony possession of a firearm. There are already large numbers of handguns in circulation in the criminal subculture. A criminal could use the same unregistered gun throughout his career and, when he "retired," he could sell or give it to a relative, friend, or criminal associate. Therefore, even a well-functioning registration system might, for many decades have little impact on the availability of handguns in the criminal subculture.

Would a new generation of criminals find it difficult to obtain unregistered handguns? Some criminals claim that it is as easy to buy a gun on the streets as it is to buy fast food. One Chicago gang member stated, "[I]t's like going through the drive-through window. 'Give me some fries, a Coke, and a 9-millimeter.'" The 500,000 firearms that are stolen each year provide an enormous pool of handguns that, even under Brady II, could not be traced to their new owners. Rifles and shotguns that are cut down could not be traced because they are not subject to registration. Criminals might also be able to purchase unmarked handguns that are smuggled into this country from abroad. Some number of never-registered handguns would, of course, continue to be sold by gun dealers, drug dealers, and gun owners hostile to the idea of handgun registration. . . .

Even if all ineligible persons could be prevented from obtaining handguns *from FFLs*, enforcing a licensing scheme in the secondary market would require a herculean enforcement effort. One reason to be pessimistic is the existence of tens of millions of unregistered handguns currently in private hands. Were it ever to appear likely that Congress was going to pass Brady II, there would almost certainly be a rush to buy handguns before the registration system became effective, just as there was a rush to buy handguns before Brady's five-day waiting period went into effect, and a rush to buy assault rifles before new sales were banned. By the time Brady II took effect, there would likely be more than 100 million handguns in private hands, perhaps millions stockpiled for future sales at a large premium. The regulatory tools, enforcement resources, and political consensus for licensing and registration on this scale simply does not exist.

9

Ballistic Fingerprinting Can Help Reduce Crime

Dianne Feinstein

Dianne Feinstein is a Democratic senator from California.

Every firearm leaves unique markings on discharged bullets and shell casings. Law enforcement agencies can use these markings, called ballistic fingerprints, to identify the gun from which the bullets came, and, eventually, track down the owner of that gun. However, just as a suspect's fingerprints must be on file for fingerprints found at a crime scene to be of any use, so too must the ballistic fingerprints of a gun be recorded *before* the gun is used to commit a crime. The federal government should pass legislation requiring the ballistic fingerprints of all newly manufactured guns to be entered into a national database that will be available to law enforcement agencies throughout the country.

Imagine if a technology existed that could help law enforcement take a single bullet from the scene of a homicide and track down the murder weapon—and then the murderer. Imagine that this technology did not require a government database of gun owners.

Well, this technology, known as ballistics fingerprinting, exists today and has already been used on a limited basis to help track down and prosecute suspects who committed crimes using a firearm.

Just as every person has a unique fingerprint, each firearm leaves unique markings on discharged bullets and shell casings. This enables law enforcement to determine if the gun from which the bullet or shell casing has been fired has been used previously in a crime, giving investigators the ability to link crimes and find suspects.

Given its potential to help law enforcement solve crimes, I believe the use of this technology should be greatly expanded and that is why I have offered legislation along with Senator Herb Kohl of Wisconsin to do just that.[1]

Unfortunately, the National Rifle Association has fought this legisla-

1. As of August 2003, Senator Feinstein's bill has not been passed into law.

Dianne Feinstein, *Mercury News*, November 19, 2002.

tion, saying that ballistics fingerprinting is an unproven, unworkable technology.

But this is simply not the case. Ballistic fingerprints from evidence found at crime scenes are being entered into the database across the country, and this has helped law enforcement solve crimes and bring criminals to justice.

Expanding the database of ballistics fingerprints will give law enforcement agencies a powerful investigative tool.

In Boston [in 2001], for instance, law enforcement was able to connect three weapons seized from several suspects to at least 15 shootings spanning several jurisdictions in two states.

In July [2002] in Louisiana, a suspect arrested for theft of a firearm was quickly connected to an armed robbery and carjacking murder he committed after stealing the firearm, because law enforcement had recovered cartridge casings from each crime scene and linked them to the stolen gun found in the suspect's possession.

Using a networked database containing more than 867,000 "fingerprint" images of shell casings and bullets, investigators were able to link evidence found at the scene of the crime with evidence found at other crime scenes and build a stronger case against the perpetrators.

And nationally, these images have resulted in almost 12,000 "hits," in which a ballistic fingerprint from one crime is matched with the fingerprint from another crime or from a firearm included in the network. Numerous violent crimes have been solved as a result of this nationwide network.

Expanding the database

The problem with this system—and the reason it cannot be used broadly today—is that only bullets and shell casings found at crime scenes, or otherwise obtained by investigators, are being entered into the database. This means that ballistic fingerprints from the millions of weapons sold in the United States each year are not included in the database.

For ballistic fingerprinting to be effective on a large scale, it is necessary to increase the number of images in the database, and the proposal I offered with Senator Kohl would do this.

Specifically, the legislation would require that ballistic fingerprints from all newly manufactured and imported firearms are entered into this national ballistics database.

Every new gun would be "fingerprinted" before a manufacturer ships the gun out of the factory, and that fingerprint would immediately be entered into the National Integrated Ballistic Information Network, which is already operating throughout the nation.

This ballistics database does not include information about the gun owner. It merely records the make, model and serial number of the firearm, along with the unique ballistic fingerprint of the firearm.

The legislation would also provide funding to assist manufacturers in establishing this system.

By recording the ballistic fingerprints of all newly manufactured and imported firearms, the system will eventually contain a large portion of the firearms used in crimes, because a large percentage of crimes are committed with relatively new guns.

According to the Bureau of Alcohol, Tobacco and Firearms, the average "time-to-crime" of a firearm in this country—in other words, how long it takes from manufacture until use—ranges between a few months to six years, depending on the type of crime. So even though many old guns may never be included in the system, a large percentage of the guns used in crime will be.

Some will argue that no ballistics fingerprint system is infallible, and that these unique fingerprints can be altered or may wear down over time. All of this is true, and nobody argues that this bill would be a panacea for gun crime in the United States—nothing is.

But there can be no doubt that expanding the database of ballistics fingerprints will give law enforcement agencies a powerful investigative tool.

10

Ballistic Fingerprinting Will Not Help Reduce Crime

Stephen P. Halbrook

Stephen P. Halbrook practices law in Virginia and is the author of That Every Man Be Armed *and* Freedmen, the Fourteenth Amendment, and the Right to Bear Arms, 1866–1876.

In the aftermath of the fall 2002 Washington, D.C., area sniper shootings, in which ten people were killed, many lawmakers began advocating legislation that would require ballistics testing of all newly manufactured firearms, supposedly to aid law enforcement agencies in tracing guns used at crime scenes. However, the technical problems that still plague ballistic fingerprinting, as well as the fact that the law ignores the millions of firearms already on the streets, ensure that the proposed legislation will do little to reduce crime. Instead, the proposed law would be used as the first step toward creating a national gun registry, which would be used to monitor, harass, and eventually disarm law-abiding citizens.

Apprehending the snipers who [in fall 2002] terrorized the Washington area took place through old-fashioned gumshoe police work and citizen involvement. That did not, however, prevent the murders from sparking a new gun-control debate, this time over whether firearms should be "fingerprinted" through use of ballistic imaging.

The hijackers of September 11, 2002, armed with box cutters and then with airliners, proved terrorists don't need firearms. John Allen Muhammad and John Lee Malvo were vocal sympathizers of the hijackers. Muhammad told Harjeet Singh that he planned to shoot a fuel tanker and cause it to explode on the freeway, and then to snipe at motorists. He also intended to kill a police officer and then blow up the mourners at the funeral home. Last June [2002], Singh disclosed these conversations to police and an FBI agent, who did nothing.

Media discussion highlights that Muhammad had been in the U.S. military and had rifle training, and that the great satan—the National Rifle Association (NRA)—has blocked "commonsense" gun legislation. Muhammad's terrorist sympathies and plans are barely mentioned.

Stephen P. Halbrook, "Symposium: Does the United States Need a Database for National Ballistic Fingerprints? No: Don't Start a Boondoggle Bullet Library That Will Become a Stealth Gun Registry," *Insight on the News*, vol. 18, November 26, 2002, p. 46. Copyright © 2003 by News World Communications, Inc. Reproduced by permission.

During the same period that the snipers played their deadly game, drug traffickers firebombed the Baltimore row house of a neighborhood antidrug activist, killing her, her husband and her five children. These murders prompted zero legislative panaceas.

But, for those focused on the single-minded agenda of regulating American citizens who own firearms, the serial sniper rejuvenated S 3096, the Ballistics, Law Assistance and Safety Technology Act, sponsored by Senators Herb Kohl (D-Wis.), Dianne Feinstein (D-Calif.), Charles Schumer (D-N.Y.) and Jack Reed (D-R.I.); and HR 408, sponsored by Representatives Anna Eshoo (D-Calif.) and John Conyers (D-Mich.). This legislation would require ballistics testing of all firearms manufactured.

Technically, [ballistic fingerprinting] just isn't feasible as a crime-fighting tool.

The bills would require manufacturers and importers to test-fire all firearms, prepare ballistics images of the bullets and cartridge casings (which must then be stored) and provide the records to the Bureau of Alcohol, Tobacco and Firearms (ATF) for its computerized database which law-enforcement agencies can access. Agencies will work with industry "to curb firearm-related crime and illegal firearm trafficking." The bills allocate $20 million to get things started.

The bills end with an unlikely section entitled "Privacy Rights of Law Abiding Citizens," which provides that ballistics information "may not be used for prosecutorial purposes unless law-enforcement officials have a reasonable belief that a crime has been committed and that ballistics information would assist in the investigation of that crime." Indeed not, prosecutions cannot proceed without probable cause to believe these things. This does not restrict surveillance of law-abiding citizens where no prosecution has been initiated.

Expensive and ineffective

The scheme is a giant loophole if it does not include the names of the current owners of the 260 million firearms already out there, who must bring their guns in for testing. To be enforceable, felony penalties must be imposed for noncompliance. The gun owners may as well be fingerprinted and photographed while they're at it —the lack of which is just another loophole. Would criminals, after they obtain their guns through theft or the black market, keep ATF current with their names, addresses and gun descriptions?

Technically, the proposal just isn't feasible as a crime-fighting tool. Fingerprints and DNA do not change, but bullets and shell casings certainly do. Rifling marks on a bullet change as the barrel receives more wear and tear—a couple of scrapes with a file can change the "fingerprint" immediately—and barrels may easily be replaced. Shell-casing marks are made by the breech face or bolt, extractor, ejector and firing pin. Again, a swipe with a file, normal wear or parts replacement creates a new "fingerprint." Ammunition made by different manufacturers give dissimilar images. Shotguns shoot ball shot through a smooth bore, so there's no bullet to test; revolvers and single-shot rifles leave no ejection marks. Only semiautomatics eject shell casings, but a brass catcher can be attached. A criminal could leave someone else's fired brass (perhaps from a shooting range) at a crime scene.

To be sure, ballistics testing can be useful on a limited basis to help solve crimes, chiefly when a crime gun is seized. A shell casing from the seized firearm may be compared with a casing from the scene of an unsolved crime. After a close match is found through use of the database, an examiner then must make visual comparisons using optical devices. By limiting the database to crime guns, the evidence is pinpointed, and the system is not overloaded with images of casings from countless firearms held by the public at large. The National Integrated Ballistic Information Network (NIBIN), administered by the ATF, conducts this type of testing.

The Bureau of Forensic Services of the California Department of Justice conducted tests and concluded: "When applying this technology to the concept of mass sampling of manufactured firearms, a huge inventory of potential candidates will be generated for manual review. This study indicates that this number of candidate cases will be so large as to be impractical and likely will create logistic complications so great that they can not be effectively addressed." A database of shell casings from all firearms would generate so many "hits" that the information would be useless.

The proposal for universal ballistic fingerprinting is just one more scheme to register, regulate and potentially incarcerate law-abiding firearm owners.

The Ballistic Imaging Evaluation and Study Act (HR 3941 and S 2581), sponsored in the U.S. House of Representatives by Republican Representative Melissa Hart of Pennsylvania and in the Senate by Democratic Senator Zell Miller of Georgia, would provide for further study by the National Academy of Sciences. The bills are supported by the NRA and the National Shooting Sports Foundation.

Maryland and New York are the only states which require ballistic imaging for all new handguns sold in those states. Neither has solved a single crime with these programs. After defunding programs that put cops on the beat, Maryland spent $5 million to test 2000 handgun shell casings. As the sniper struck in the D.C. suburbs, the FBI disclosed that Maryland had halted certain background checks on gun buyers because funds had run out.

When the sniper was on the loose, we saw an illustration of how police are spread too thin when every citizen is a suspect. While cops halted all traffic to search white vans, ATF went into every gun store in the Maryland suburbs and got the identity of every purchaser of a .223-caliber rifle. Cops then beat on the doors of every such person—there were hundreds—and seized the rifles for ballistic testing. All the while the sniper cruised around in his blue Chevy Caprice sedan with his rifle purchased on the West Coast.

While current bills in Congress would require ballistic testing only of new guns, the system would be worthless without testing of all guns and registration of all gun owners. Any transfer of a gun would require notice to ATF. The replacement of any parts, whether a barrel or firing pin, would necessitate new ballistic testing. Thus, the sale of firearm replacement parts would need to be regulated—they would need serial numbers and would require an ATF permit to acquire. New crimes with new felony penalties must be legislated.

The above is not a slippery-slope prediction; rather it is the only logical path of the current push for governmental omniscience regarding gun owners. Every new control has inherent "loopholes" allowing "circumvention" and these defects will continue until perfect knowledge by the authorities is attained. Gun controllers insist that knowing who owns every gun and the fingerprints of every gun would have led police immediately to Muhammad. As claimed by the Brady Campaign to Prevent Gun Violence, ballistic fingerprinting would have "solved this crime after the first shooting."

Yet, in all but one of the shootings, no shell casing was found since Muhammad and/or Malvo were shooting from inside a car trunk, where there were openings for the barrel and the scope. The casings were ejected into the trunk. Perhaps the Brady group will suggest a further panacea—making it illegal to shoot from car trunks.

While prohibitionist groups deny that ballistic-fingerprinting programs would require registration of firearm owners, they simultaneously are calling for bans on ordinary rifles. More typically—as experiences from Nazi Germany to current England and New York City verify—registration is enacted first, and then confiscation. Today's approach is more direct: "Tougher restrictions must be placed on so-called sniper rifles, such as the .50, .308 and .223 calibers," says Tom Diaz of the Violence Policy Center. Representative John Conyers (D-Mich.) urges the Federal Trade Commission to investigate the marketing of rifles to civilians, arguing that "Sniper weapons are different from standard hunting rifles because they are designed to strike a target from a distance."

Factually, the .308 is a "high-caliber" rifle that hunters typically equip with a scope to strike deer "from a distance." The .223 rifle is the most popular caliber for varmint hunting. "Sniper" rifle is a pejorative substitute for "hunting" rifle.

Since only one shot was fired in each of the D.C. area murders, the murder weapon could have just as well been a single-shot. In fact it was a Bushmaster XM 15 semiautomatic. Contrary to media reports, that rifle is not an "assault weapon" as defined by federal law. Yet prohibitionists already are appealing to the recent killing spree to argue for reenactment of the federal assault-weapon ban which sunsets in 2004.

The proposal for universal ballistic fingerprinting is just one more scheme to register, regulate and potentially incarcerate law-abiding firearm owners. It offers no true benefit for law enforcement—as the Fraternal Order of Police puts it: "With such small chances that it would be used to solve a firearm crime . . . these are law-enforcement dollars best spent elsewhere." Instead of pinpointing likely suspects, it overextends the net and makes a suspect out of every American citizen who chooses to own a firearm.

[Editor's note: As of August 2003, none of the pending legislation discussed in this viewpoint has been passed into law.]

Organizations to Contact

The editors have compiled the following list of organizations concerned with the issues debated in this book. The descriptions are derived from materials provided by the organizations. All have publications or information available for interested readers. The list was compiled on the date of publication of the present volume; the information provided here may change. Be aware that many organizations take several weeks or longer to respond to inquiries, so allow as much time as possible.

American Civil Liberties Union (ACLU)
132 W. 43rd St., New York, NY 10036
(212) 944-9800 • fax: (212) 869-9065
website: www.aclu.org

The ACLU champions the rights set forth in the Declaration of Independence and the U.S. Constitution. The ACLU interprets the Second Amendment as a guarantee for states to form militias, not as a guarantee of the individual right to own and bear firearms. Consequently, the organization believes that gun control is constitutional and, since guns are dangerous, it is necessary. The ACLU publishes the semiannual *Civil Liberties* in addition to policy statements and reports.

Americans for Gun Safety (AGS) and the AGS Foundation
(202) 775-0300 • fax: (202) 775-0430
website: www.americansforgunsafety.com • www.agsfoundation.com

Founded in 2000, AGS is a nonpartisan, not-for-profit advocacy organization that supports the rights of law-abiding gun owners and promotes reasonable and effective proposals for fighting gun crime and keeping guns out of the hands of criminals and children. The organization's top priorities are closing America's gun show loophole, improving the background check system for gun purchases, encouraging better enforcement of current gun laws, and promoting gun safety. The AGS Foundation provides background, research, and reference materials to the public and to policymakers on issues relating to gun safety, such as the reports *Broken Records: How America's Faulty Background Check System Allows Criminals to Get Guns* and *Stolen Guns: Arming the Enemy*.

Brady Campaign to Prevent Gun Violence and Brady Center to Prevent Gun Violence
1225 Eye St. NW, Suite 1100, Washington, DC 20005
(202) 898-0792 • fax: (202) 289-7319
website: www.bradycampaign.org • www.bradycenter.com

The Brady Campaign to Prevent Gun Violence was formerly known as Handgun Control, Inc. The campaign works to enact and enforce sensible gun laws, regulations, and public policies through grassroots activism, electing pro-gun control public officials, and increasing public awareness of gun violence. The Brady Center works to reform the gun industry and educate the public about gun violence through litigation and grassroots mobilization and to enact and enforce sensible regulations to reduce gun violence, including regulations governing the gun industry. The Brady Campaign website offers dozens of issue briefs, fact sheets, legislative updates, and links to news stories on gun control.

Cato Institute
1000 Massachusetts Ave. NW, Washington, DC 20001
(202) 842-0200 • fax: (202) 842-3490
website: www.cato.org

The Cato Institute is a libertarian public-policy research foundation. It evaluates government policies and offers reform proposals and commentary on its website. Its publications include the Cato Policy Analysis series of reports, including "Pistol Whipped: Baseless Lawsuits, Foolish Laws," "Fighting Back: Crime, Self-Defense, and the Right to Carry a Handgun," and "Trust the People: The Case Against Gun Control." It also publishes the magazine *Regulation*, the *Cato Policy Report*, and books such as *The Samurai, the Mountie, and the Cowboy: Should America Adopt the Gun Controls of Other Democracies?*

Citizens Committee for the Right to Keep and Bear Arms
12500 NE Tenth Pl., Bellevue, WA 98005
(206) 454-4911 • fax: (206) 451-3959
website: www.ccrkba.org

The committee believes that the U.S. Constitution's Second Amendment guarantees and protects the right of individual Americans to own guns. It works to educate the public concerning this right and to lobby legislators to prevent the passage of gun control laws. The committee is affiliated with the Second Amendment Foundation and has more than six hundred thousand members. It publishes several magazines, including *Point Blank*, which is available online, as well as *Gun Week, Women & Guns,* and *Gun News Digest.*

Coalition to Stop Gun Violence (CSGV)
1000 16th St. NW, Suite 603, Washington, DC 20002
(202) 530-0340 • fax: (202) 530-0331
website: www.csgv.org

The CSGV lobbies at the local, state, and federal levels to ban the sale of handguns to individuals and to institute licensing and registration of all firearms. It also litigates cases against firearms makers. Its publications include various informational sheets on gun violence and the *Annual Citizens' Conference to Stop Gun Violence Briefing Book*, a compendium of gun control fact sheets, arguments, and resources.

Independence Institute
14142 Denver West Pkwy., Suite 101, Golden, CO 80401
(303) 279-6536 • fax: (303) 279-4176
website: www.i2i.org

The Independence Institute is a pro–free market think tank that supports gun ownership as both a civil liberty and a constitutional right. Its publications include issue papers opposing gun control, as well as the book *Gun Control and Gun Rights: A Reader and Guide*. Its website also contains articles, fact sheets, and commentary from a variety of sources.

Jews for the Preservation of Firearms Ownership (JPFO)
PO Box 270143, Hartford, WI 53027
(262) 673-9745 • fax: (262) 673-9746
website: www.jpfo.org

JPFO is an educational organization that believes Jewish law mandates self-defense. Its primary goal is the elimination of the idea that gun control is a socially useful public policy in any country. JPFO publishes the quarterly *Firearms Sentinel*, the booklet *Will "Gun Control" Make You Safer?*, and regular news alerts.

Million Mom March Foundation
San Francisco General Hospital, San Francisco, CA 94110
toll free: (800) RINGING
website: www.millionmommarch.org

Formerly the Bell Campaign, the Million Mom March Foundation is a grassroots organization that supports common sense gun laws. The foundation organized the Million Mom March, in which thousands marched through Washington, D.C., on Mother's Day, May 14, 2000, in support of licensing and registration and other firearm regulations. The foundation's website provides fact sheets on gun violence and gun control initiatives.

National Crime Prevention Council (NCPC)
1700 K St. NW, 2nd Fl., Washington, DC 20006-3817
(202) 466-6272 • fax: (202) 296-1356
website: www.ncpc.org

NCPC is a branch of the U.S. Department of Justice. Through its programs and educational materials, the council works to teach Americans how to reduce crime and to address its causes. It provides readers with information on gun control and gun violence. NCPC's publications include the newsletter *Catalyst*, which is published ten times a year, and the book *Reducing Gun Violence: What Communities Can Do*.

National Organization for Victim Assistance (NOVA)
1757 Park Rd. NW, Washington, DC 20010
(202) 232-6682 • toll free: (800) TRY-NOVA • fax: (202) 462-2255
website: www.try-nova.org

NOVA serves as a national forum for victim advocacy by assisting victims of crime, providing education and technical assistance to those who assist victims, and serving as a membership organization for supporters of the victims movement. NOVA publishes the monthly *NOVA Newsletter*.

National Rifle Association of America (NRA)
11250 Waples Mill Rd., Fairfax, VA 22030
(703) 267-1000 • fax: (703) 267-3989
website: www.nra.org

With nearly three million members, the NRA is America's largest organization of gun owners. It is also the primary lobbying group for those who oppose gun control laws. The NRA believes that such laws violate the U.S. Constitution and do nothing to reduce crime. In addition to its monthly magazine, *America's First Freedom, American Rifleman, American Hunter, InSights,* and *Shooting Sports USA*, the NRA publishes numerous books, bibliographies, reports, and pamphlets on gun ownership, gun safety, and gun control.

Second Amendment Foundation
12500 NE Tenth Pl., Bellevue, WA 98005
(206) 454-7012 • fax: (206) 451-3959
website: www.saf.org

The foundation is dedicated to informing Americans about their Second Amendment right to keep and bear firearms. It believes that gun control laws violate this right. The foundation publishes numerous books, including *The Amazing Vanishing Second Amendment, The Best Defense: True Stories of Intended Victims Who Defended Themselves with a Firearm*, and *CCW: Carrying Concealed Weapons*. The complete text of the book *How to Defend Your Gun Rights* is available on its website.

U.S. Department of Justice, Bureau of Justice Statistics
810 Seventh St. NW, Washington, DC 20531
(202) 307-0756
website: www.ojp.usdoj.gov/bjs

The Department of Justice protects citizens by maintaining effective law enforcement, crime prevention, crime detection, and prosecution and rehabilitation of offenders. The Bureau of Justice Statistics offers key figures on gun crimes through its website and through publications such as *Firearm Injury and Death from Crime, 1993–97*.

Violence Policy Center
2000 P St. NW, Suite 200, Washington, DC 20036
(202) 822-8200 • fax: (202) 822-8202
website: www.vpc.org

The center is an educational foundation that conducts research on firearms violence. It works to educate the public concerning the dangers of guns and supports gun control measures. The center's publications include the reports *Handgun Licensing and Registration: What It Can and Cannot Do, Credit Card Armies: Firearms and Training for Terror in the United States, Sitting Ducks: The Threat to the Chemical and Refinery Industry from .50 Caliber Sniper Rifles*, and *Where'd They Get Their Guns? An Analysis of the Firearms Used in High-Profile Shootings, 1963 to 2001*.

Bibliography

Books

Alfred Blumstein and Joel Wallman	*The Crime Drop in America.* New York: Cambridge University Press, 2000.
John M. Bruce and Clyde Wilcox	*The Changing Politics of Gun Control.* Lanham, MD: Rowman & Littlefield, 1998.
Philip J. Cook and Jens Ludwig	*Gun Violence: The Real Costs.* New York: Oxford University Press, 2000.
Vic Cox	*Guns, Violence, and Teens.* Springfield, NJ: Enslow, 1997.
Jennifer Croft	*Everything You Need to Know About Guns in the Home.* New York: Rosen, 2000.
Alexander DeConde	*Gun Violence in America: The Struggle for Control.* Boston: Northeastern University Press, 2001.
Tom Diaz	*Making a Killing: The Business of Guns in America.* New York: New Press, 1999.
Jan E. Dizard, Robert Merril Muth, and Stephen P. Andrews Jr., eds.	*Guns in America: A Reader.* New York: New York University Press, 1999.
Wilbur Edel	*Gun Control: Threat to Liberty or Defense Against Anarchy?* Westport, CT: Praeger, 1995.
George A. Gellert	*Confronting Violence: Answers to Questions About the Epidemic Destroying America's Homes and Communities.* Boulder, CO: Westview Press, 1997.
James Gilligan	*Violence: Our Deadly Epidemic and Its Causes.* New York: G.P. Putnam, 1996.
James B. Jacobs	*Can Gun Control Work?* New York: Oxford University Press, 2002.
Gary Kleck	*Targeting Guns: Firearms and Their Control.* New York: de Gruyter, 1997.
Gary Kleck and Don B. Kates Jr.	*Armed: New Perspectives on Gun Control.* Amherst, NY: Prometheus Books, 2001.
Wayne R. LaPierre	*Guns, Crime, and Freedom.* New York: HarperPerennial, 1995.
John R. Lott Jr.	*More Guns, Less Crime: Understanding Crime and Gun-Control Laws.* New York: New York University Press, 2002.

Andrew McClurg, Dave Kopel, and Brandon Denning	*Gun Control and Gun Rights: A Reader and Guide.* New York: New York University Press, 2002.
Maryann Miller	*Working Together Against Gun Violence.* New York: Rosen, 1997.
Ted Schwarz	*Kids and Guns: The History, the Present, the Dangers, and the Remedies.* New York: Franklin Watts, 1999.
Joseph F. Sheley	*In the Line of Fire: Youth, Guns, and Violence in Urban America.* New York: de Gruyter, 1995.
Peter Squires	*Gun Culture or Gun Control: Firearms, Violence, and Society.* New York: Routledge, 2000.
Josh Sugarmann	*Every Handgun Is Aimed at You: The Case for Banning Handguns.* New York: New Press, 2001.
William Weir	*A Well-Regulated Militia: The Battle over Gun Control.* North Haven, CT: Archon, 1997.
Franklin E. Zimring and Gordon Hawkins	*Crime Is Not the Problem: Lethal Violence in America.* New York: Oxford University Press, 1997.

Periodicals

Matt Bai	"A Gun Deal's Fatal Wound," *Newsweek*, February 5, 2001.
Steve Bonta	"Gun Grab Revival," *New American*, February 11, 2002.
Sarah Brady and John R. Lott Jr.	"Would New Requirements for Gun Buyers Save Lives?" *Insight on the News*, June 21, 1999.
H. Sterling Burnett	"Suing Gun Manufacturers: The Protection of Lawful Commerce in Arms," *Vital Speeches of the Day*, June 15, 2002.
Business Week	"Say Yes to Serious Gun Control," August 16, 1999.
Fox Butterfield	"FBI Study Finds Gun Use in Violent Crimes Declining," *New York Times*, October 18, 1999.
Nicholas Confessore	"Control Freaks," *American Prospect*, April 8, 2002.
Congressional Digest	"Firearms in America: The Link Between Guns and Violence," November 1999.
Richard F. Corlin	"The Secrets of Gun Violence in America," *Vital Speeches of the Day*, August 1, 2001.
Economist	"Economic Focus: Gun Control and Crime," January 13, 2001.
Thomas R. Eddlem	"Their Target: Your Guns," *New American*, October 7, 2002.
Justin Ewers	"Choose a Weapon," *U.S. News & World Report*, February 10, 2003.
Laura Helmuth	"Has America's Tide of Violence Receded for Good?" *Science*, July 28, 2000.

Issues and Controversies On File	"Gun Control," July 14, 2000.
Bronwyn Jones	"Arming Myself with a Gun Is Not the Answer," *Newsweek*, May 22, 2000.
John R. Lott Jr.	"Bullets and Bunkum: The Futility of 'Ballistic Fingerprinting,'" *National Review*, November 11, 2002.
John R. Lott Jr.	"When Gun Control Costs Lives," *National Forum*, Fall 2000.
Sam MacDonald	"Gun Control's New Language: How Anti-Terror Rhetoric Is Being Used Against the Second Amendment," *Reason*, March 2002.
Joyce Lee Malcolm	"Gun Control's Twisted Outcome: Restricting Firearms Has Helped Make England More Crime-Ridden than the U.S.," *Reason*, November 2002.
Gary Rosen	"Yes and No to Gun Control," *Commentary*, September 2000.
Noam Scheiber	"Gun Shy," *New Republic*, January 29, 2001.
Susan B. Sorenson	"Regulating Firearms as a Consumer Product," *Science*, November 19, 1999.
Thomas Sowell	"Gun-Control Crowd Misuses Fear Factor to Distort the Truth," *Insight on the News*, November 12, 2002.
Time	"Dodging the Bullet," November 4, 2002.
Douglas S. Weil	"Closing Gun Control Loopholes," *National Forum*, Fall 2000.

Index

77